The Ascension Primer

The Ascension Primer

Karen Bishop

~ *Dedication* ~

This book is dedicated to all those experiencing the ascension process. Your courage, spirit and dedication are truly making a difference for every living thing in the cosmos.

Also by Karen Bishop

Remembering Your Soul Purpose : A Part Of Ascension

TABLE OF CONTENTS

Introduction

IT IS MY DESIRE that this book will serve to activate within you what you already know. Learning through direct experience is really the only way I know to evolve, grow, and learn anything new. Through experience, we really get it. We feel it, know it, and believe it because we are getting it at all levels. Experience creates a great "aha!" It enables us to finally really know and understand some of what we may have read or heard before. It creates information with a very new and deep meaning as we have then *been* it. Experience creates the state of *being* that many of us are finding to be most certainly a way of the higher realms.

Through experience, we may also find that much of what we have read regarding spiritual matters was simply inaccurate. I have found through my own personal ascension process that the majority of what has been written and taught is absolutely not how it is in the higher realms. This is the beauty of personal experience.

This book is about the ascension process. Beginning in the year 2000, many individuals (which will be referred to here as "lightworkers") began experiencing very intense, strange, unworldly, and uncomprehendable mental, emotional, physical, and spiritual "symptoms" and life occurrences. These occurrences and symptoms may have been experienced in years past in moderation by a very few spiritual seekers, but the year 2000 really accelerated things. Many, many more individuals were involved in the process and the process was unfolding at a very rapid and intense rate.

Very generally speaking, the ascension process is an evolutionary process that involves the raising of human consciousness, which will result in the creation of a much more highly evolved planet and a much more highly evolved human. As the ascension process continues, the inhabitants of the earth will "ascend" through the human body and return to Source, or the Creator.

The lightworkers were born on the planet Earth at this particular time with a very specific plan in mind. (More details about this plan are included further along in this book.) And although it may at times seem otherwise to them, the lightworkers are the masters here...the stars of the show...the power behind and within the ascension process. They are paving the way for all to follow...here on Earth, as well as within the entire universe. The ascension process, therefore, is a great honor and amazing one-of-a-kind experience. Lightworkers are highly revered throughout the cosmos for their dedication and willingness to have this experience and to serve.

If you are one who has been experiencing strange physical anomalies, do not know who you are looking at in the mirror, feel as though you are having some kind of mental breakdown and may be losing your mind (you are, you know), have lost your job, your friends or your family, or are very simply going through major and rapid transitions, then this book is for you. For anyone going through the ascension process, it is something that our souls will never forget. At soul levels we consider this experience to be a very special addition to our resumé. As physical vessels for using and experiencing energy, which is the purpose for existence, the ascension process, therefore, is an incredible and rare experience for us.

My wish is that this book will validate for you what you have experienced so far, as well as activating within you what you may not consciously remember...but your soul does! At your deepest levels, may you remember your soul plan as you read the pages of this book.

Wishing you heaven in your heart, starlight in your soul, and miracles in your life during these miraculous times. God bless and happy reading,

Karen

Foreword

"GOOD-BYE MOM!" a young boy calls out as he leaves his home one morning. Eager to go out and play, he finds himself approaching a group of children, already involved in a game of their own. As he enters their game of make-believe, he contributes his own special energy to the drama they are creating. Out of the corner of his eye, he sees another very exciting game transpiring in the field near-by. Not wanting to leave the fun game he is currently playing, but wanting to experience more, he magically leaves a part of himself there, and then proceeds onward, excited to become involved in the activities at the near-by field. As he continues on with his day, he is drawn to more and more areas of fun and exciting games, where he becomes involved in each one, spreading himself far and wide. Sometimes, he joins the games of others and helps them to create exciting and fun dramas. Other times he begins his own creation, and eventually other children come to play. After awhile, he becomes very weary. He has experienced much, and desires to go home.

A deep part of him knows that he is done playing for a while. It is growing dark and he is ready for Mom's dinner and a warm bed. All this experiencing and playing is not as fun as it was in the beginning and he is VERY TIRED. Being so tired and gone for so long, he has forgotten how to get himself back home. He doesn't think he can make it back on his own, and is very frightened to leave all the games he has been playing, as that is all he can remember. It has been a long day, and now as well as being tired and weary, he is feeling very lost. To help himself get back home, he says good-bye to all the parts of himself in the other games. He tells them they can go on and find their own fun without him. Finally, his weariness wins out. As he completely lets go and quits trying to get back home on his own, he lies down on some grass. He hears his mother calling, "Time to come home!" and knows he is near. As he lies there in fatigue and surrender, totally letting go and trusting that his mother will come for him, a strange thing happens. Above him he hears his mother's voice. "You can come home now, or I can bring you a nice hot dinner and warm bed right there, and you can start over and create a brand new game right there where you began your first one." Should he go back home to his mother's house where he first originated? Or should he stay in this state of purification that he has found himself in after shedding so much of his prior incarnations, and start again in a New World with brand New experiences?

And then he notices another strange occurrence. He does not seem to be the only one going home. In the past, he remembers going home when he has become weary, but all by himself. This time, all the kids in the neighborhood are going home all at once, and in one big group, at the same time he is. And they are all deciding if they should create a brand new game right there on Earth, with all the comforts of home, or go all the way back to Mom's house.

Just as this young boy is doing, we are getting ready to go home. As we made our first journey away from the Creator (Mom's house), we were shot out into the universe as a beautiful spark of Source energy. Eventually, we infused our energy (incarnated) into many places, having many multidimensional experiences, and all at the same time. I can remember my first experience of creating planets (and maybe you can too) as an outlet and game for creation. Pulling together all the elements needed was an exciting learning experience, and even then, I missed the comfort and security of "home". As we have infused our energy into as many places as we could, creating as many scenarios and having as many experiences as we chose to, we have finally experienced enough, and are ready to return to Source and start over. This time arrives for each soul eventually, but what is distinctly different about our current experience of ascension, is that we are going en masse.

In August of 2005 we finally reached critical mass on planet Earth. This meant that enough inhabitants of the planet were vibrating at a higher level or in other words had raised their consciousness to a higher level, therefore assisting the planet in now reaching this higher level as a whole. We could now ascend as a planet.

Then, in January of 2006 we were given the opportunity to jump across to the other side (or to begin residing in a higher dimension, to live without the veil, or whichever explanation you resonate with the most). This was a critical and pivotal time as there were many lightworkers and many inhabitants of the planet who made other choices, and chose to stay back or to move on to other realities that better matched the current evolution of their souls.

So what started this ascension process, what does it involve, what does it really mean, and how are each of us being affected?

1

ASCENSION DEFINED

SEVERAL YEARS AGO I gave soul readings to individuals. I especially enjoyed this activity as it continually placed me in the higher realms, viewing things from the soul level. One of my favorite activities is going back to the origin of things, or where it all began...going to the highest and deepest levels...the places where the illusions of the lower dimensions do not exist. It is truly a beautiful place.

Each of these soul readings was distinctly unique according to the individual I was interacting with. But there was one thread that everyone had in common. Each and every person was here from a star or planet (and a few from the nature realm) with a unique and distinct vibration or identity. And within this vibration or identity came the special purpose and contribution that each individual was here to express and share.

The Who's Who Party

Every star or planet has its' own distinct vibration or purpose and they are all vastly different. Some individuals I read for were here from stars that were very nearby and some were here from places that were very, very far away. Many had never even inhabited this planet Earth before. Some of these individuals were so highly sensitive that I wondered how they were truly surviving on this planet during this time. They found that they had become near recluses as the outside world and what it brought was much too harsh for them.

One individual was here from a planet where everything existed as gliding and soaring blobs of color. It looked like a rainbow planet, very evolved with a high, refined energy of color and beauty. The purpose and vibration of this planet was to bring beauty, joy, and love to all it encountered. So here, then, existed a place refined down to the energy of using color as a way of being and a center of existence. This particular woman was currently an artist. She would also be able to heal or balance through the process of light moving through a prism of color, if she chose. This, for her, was how she resonated and what she would then respond to the most. Her purpose was in bringing color and its many gifts to all she encountered.

Another individual was here to show others how everything worked. The vibration of his planet was responsible for explaining and guiding all other planets and places. His planet had a totally different energy. It existed and functioned like intricate gears all working together, and very busy indeed! Lots of movement and interaction in a perfect and complex system...but this was the beauty of this particular planet and it reflected why this man was here...to show others and the world how everything worked together. At the 3D level he would be an engineer, but at the higher levels he would show others how to integrate the higher ways into their lives through harmony. Wherever he went, he continually found himself in situations that provided him opportunities to explain how things worked...and he did this so naturally!

And some individuals were here as aspects and human forms of nature. One woman was part of the tree family and used this grounding and unique vibration as a substantial and integral part of her yoga teachings. Another woman was part of the nature kingdom and had actually been the origin of the first running stream here on Earth when it was created. She had such ancient energy that communing and connecting with her deep past was incredibly expanding and uniting at the same time. Those that came from nature were here in human form as representatives of the Earth herself (as they were literally part of her) in order to educate the current inhabitants of the planet on her ways and to teach others what she was about. They knew the information well, because they *were* the Earth herself, only in human form in order for others to relate to them more fully.

The older and more highly developed stars (or planets) produced much more highly vibrating humans. So was true in the opposing direction, with the younger and closer stars bringing a younger and not as aware or highly mechanically wired human to the Earth at this time. But none-the-less, all were here for this rare and unprecedented Shift of the Ages or ascension process.

It became very clear from the soul readings what was going on and the picture of the ascension process then became even clearer. But personally experiencing and seeing this phenomenon made this aspect of the ascension process even more real. I could never have imagined that this was how it was if I hadn't experienced it for myself firsthand.

We are returning back to Source where it all began. Each and every aspect of the universe is represented here in human form to experience and complete this process, therefore reverberating it to their star families back home. Every aspect of life in the universe has sent a representative or two to go through this transmutation process here on Earth...it can only be accomplished in form. This is how consciousness expands...in form. And in addition, encountering souls from your star of origin rekindles a strong bond and familiarity, as you vibrate so similarly...with a similar purpose, of course.

And yet through my own experiences, I have come to know that each of us is also being very protected by our families from our star or nature homes. Some of these individuals who had never been on Earth before had been sent almost reluctantly by their caretakers or families from home, as they knew they must participate, but were concerned for the well-being of their offspring. These "parents" are watching very closely as they hover ever nearby making sure nothing goes awry. It is a beautiful sight to see. So if you have always felt very protected or perhaps been told by sensitives that you are very protected, this is most likely why.

Some of us here have a very different scenario going. Yes, we are being monitored by our star families as well, but we have done this type of work and service for so long, that we are simply old soldiers. We are so very used to going out and creating new planets, setting up new systems, laying new grids and so forth, that this may seem like the same old soul experience except for one thing...these individuals are experiencing the ascension process as well. Everyone and everything is returning to Source to begin again...no one escapes. This particular time on planet Earth has brought every manifestation of life together. It is truly amazing that we are all here at the same time. We were all invited to a big party by "invitation only" with great planning at the higher levels. So we dropped all of our other "activities", and arrived here with all our eggs in one basket.

So what does all this mean, exactly?

This particular universe has expanded as far as it can go and it is starting over and beginning again, and it is all happening through this beautiful blue jewel called planet Earth. Very briefly, when a soul begins its' existence, it shoots off as a spark from the original Source (or God, the Creator, or whatever your preference). Each soul then infuses its' energy or parts of itself into many different forms in order to experience and create more of itself all over the universe. We had infused our energy into many, many places, having many, many multidimensional experiences. We became tired and felt we had gone as far as we could go, and as a group, decided to call it a day. Every life form in the universe currently has representation here on Earth at this time, as the ascension process occurs through form. As each representative currently on Earth goes through this process, the transmutations are reverberated to all the aspects of each representative back "home" in order for all to benefit. And not only will our star families benefit, but at lower levels all inhabitants of planet Earth will eventually follow as we pave the way. Every form of life in the universe will be captured and go through a "turning inside out" kind of process. Like a massive cleansing at all levels and within every form out there, we are being readied for a very New beginning. We are releasing it all...all the multidimensional aspects of ourselves where we infused our energy, down to all the denser aspects of our current human selves. We are "undoing" everything that we created from the beginning in order to start anew. And our New beginning that will occur here on planet Earth will take place in a higher dimension with a higher consciousness. We are starting over indeed.

Igniting The Fire

What actually started the ascension process? Why and how did it begin?

Creation basically occurs from all sides. We have a thought or feeling which creates a manifestation. At the same time, a manifestation creates a thought or feeling. Say you are thinking of someone, and just then the phone rings. Of course, it is precisely the person you were thinking of who is on the other end of the phone. "I was just thinking of you!", you exclaim. Or you may have been thinking of someone recently and then you run into them in the store. Did you create the encounter, or did you know at a higher level that they would be coming into your space, therefore creating thoughts of them? Which comes first, the chicken or the egg? Being that there really is no linear time, everything is actually occurring at once. The most basic law of the universe is that like energies always attract like and corresponding energies...and all at the same time.

The souls of the universe were ready to play a new game and start anew. This created a summoning for a new and different manifestation to occur. Every existing thing in the universe has its' own unique vibration and purpose, including the planets. The planets and their positioning in the universe were such that they were vibrating in a way that encouraged souls to be ready to create something new. The souls were also encouraging the planets to move in directions and vibrate in ways so that they were ready to change and create something new. It came from all sides and all at once. And in addition, at lower and scientific levels, we are receiving blasts of crystalline (higher vibrating energy) from the sun in the form of solar flares. These surges of higher vibrating energy also contribute to the raising of the vibration of the earth and her inhabitants. Everything was in on this together and all going in the same direction. *Very simply*, it was just plain time for the ascension process to occur. It was time to start anew for all aspects of the universe. Remember, we are all one.

At lower levels, how does this process affect us individually?

Am I Dead Yet?

My grandmother passed away in August of 2005. She was 97 years old and we were very close. For the last year or two of her life, she was very ready to go. She wanted to be done with it, as her quality of life had deteriorated and there wasn't much that she could do anymore. She was tired. During her last year, she began to experience panic and anxiety. She certainly could not remember dying before and had no frame of reference for it. Although she wanted to "be done", she kept hanging on. Finally, around the time we reached the point of critical mass (where enough of us had agreed and were willing to give it all up and go to a higher dimension), she was finally ready to go. At her soul level, she knew she could finally leave...her job was done. For a few days she slowly slipped in and out of consciousness...sometimes she was here and sometimes she was on the other side. And then she slipped into total unconsciousness, waited until her loved ones were with other loved ones (so no one would be alone when they got the news of her passing), and totally transitioned.

For a week or so she would come and visit her loved ones. I have to say, she was so blissfully happy having released the burden of her body. And it was so very pleasant to have her at my beckoned call and be able to speak with her and enjoy her presence all the time. And then she was off to her new assignment and one that suited her to a tee. Most of the time she is busy doing her service work on the other side, but there are still times in between "assignments" when she shows up and we can spend time together. Oh, how I love my grandmother, and it is this love that enables us to stay connected so easily.

Just like the process my grandmother went through when she made her transition, we are dying as well, only *we are dying while we remain alive in a human body*. The ascension process involves transitioning to a higher dimension, and in order to do this, we are going through some strange, intense, and very uncomfortable experiences. We are letting go of just about anything and everything as part of this process. And the experiences we are having are very similar if not identical to the dying process in the old 3D reality.

When the death experience occurs in the 3D world, everything is released in one sudden whoosh! The density, burdens, illusions, and much else that we humans carried around for our entire lives is released and left behind. This is what is occurring now through the ascension process, only gradually, even though it may seem otherwise! Remember, if you are one of the many who is experiencing ascension symptoms, you are also one of the leaders and the way show-ers and your soul absolutely knew what it was getting into. At soul levels you knew you could handle it. Even though at times it may not feel like it, as the ascension process can take an extraordinary toll on a person...you are also calling the shots, even though you may not consciously be aware of it. This was the plan...lightworkers created it at the highest levels and then placed themselves into the game or drama of it all. We were excited about it. We are being stretched as far as we can possibly go during this process, in order for this transition to occur as quickly as possible. We are rarely stretched too far. We just love to whine! And in addition, all is being monitored. We are being watched over with loving eyes from the non-physical world.

At one point during the throes of my ascension process a few years ago, I was literally on the floor crying, "I can't do this! This is far too much! I am absolutely unable to go through this!" I was turning inside out, feeling incredible pain and anguish. I felt I was being stretched further than I could possibly go and experiencing more than I was able to handle. I was in a process of realigning to a higher vibration, and I can't even begin to describe it to you in words. Just then, a big beautiful non-physical being showed up and very strongly and assuredly said, "Your attitude is creating 50% more anguish than the process. You would not be going through this if you could not handle it". And that's the way it is for all of us.

We have higher non-physical beings watching over us *and* we will not be stretched further than we can go.

Paradise Rolls In

In June of 2005 an opening occurred in the Hawaiian Islands and a New (or old) energy returned. This area on the planet is where Lemuria once was. This area also extends into Southern California. Eons ago, Lemuria existed as an ancient civilization embodying the energy of the feminine...a paradise where peace, harmony, prosperity and psychic ways prevailed. This non-power oriented civilization known as Mu eventually ended.

Part of the ascension process involves a restoration of the original blueprint of the planet Earth. The original purpose of Earth was that it be a place for creating and experiencing through form. As we progress (or *regress* as we are releasing and letting go of so much) through the ascension process, we are then much more in alignment with the energy of this ancient civilization again. When the vibration of the planet reached a certain (and higher) frequency, it was time, then, for the energies of Lemuria to return. We were now in alignment with them.

Many places on the planet contain and protect the higher secrets or higher ways of the ancient and original Earth. These higher vibrating secrets were hidden and buried eons ago by some of us, as we knew what was to come and did not want them in the wrong hands. As the time was finally here in June of 2005, the Lemurian energy was again released. This energy had a lot to do with the energy of the feminine being restored. You may have felt a very strong urge at this time to travel to Hawaii. Some actually did go, while some could accomplish the same by not actually being present there. In addition, many were drawn to Southern California as well. I was in Southern California many times during this period and could really feel a very different and beautiful energy emerging there (I lived there for most of the first 36 years of my life and know the energy well). If you were one who had this strong desire to be in these locations, you were simply wanting to be present to unveil the energies and the blueprint that you had buried to protect eons ago.

When we experience an energy from higher levels, many times we feel it at a lower level as well. During this time, with *restoration* as the occurring energetic theme, many began a desire to restore their homes, their furniture, their cars or historical sites near-by, and so forth. This is how energy works because we can feel it at many different levels according to who we are and how we are wired.

So here began the restoration of the original blueprint...in the areas of the Pacific Ocean and Southern California. Many times we find ourselves going to specific geographical areas for one particular reason related to a 3D purpose, but at soul levels we know exactly where we need to be and our souls make sure we get there for one reason or another. And know that even though this blueprint began to emerge here, it continued to reverberate throughout the rest of the planet as well. Australia and New Zealand have the Lemurian energies as well, along with some incredible secrets of crystal caves!

The ascension process involves a returning back to an organic state. It involves a spinning off of all past creations. It involves a restoration to the original blueprint in order to start again. Before we start anew, we must lay a basic organic foundation and then go from there.

As I write these words in March of 2006, I currently reside in a fairly remote area in the mountains of Northeastern Arizona surrounded on three sides by very nearby sites of ancient ruins. My current passion, purpose, role, and desire is in bringing in the presence of higher vibrating star beings for regular interaction and involvement with the planet and our society...as a way of living and being in regular communion with them. This is the way of societies and planets with a higher vibration and higher consciousness and what we are rapidly evolving into. Through regular interaction and communication, they are telling me how the ancients used to commune with them. They are showing me how important alignments are...alignments with the stars and the sun and moon at specific times to create portals or openings for them to enter and merge with us. What is occurring here is a return to the ancient and original ways where this was done. It is part of the process of returning to an original and more purified state (organic) of communing with higher level beings.

And at lower levels, many more are being guided to eat organic. My mother recently told me that Wal-Mart will now be offering organic foods. Just another manifestation of returning to the original and purer state of things before we can move forward. What I am saying here is that we will first restore, going back to a simple, clean and clear state, and then take creation further than the Lemurian energies and certainly further than the energies of Atlantis. Once the basic foundation is laid, we can then create whatever we choose. Remember, we are beginning again, fresh and new, and can create a planet that will be whatever we choose it to be.

Because we are truly starting over, and because WE are the current and basically New residents here on the New Earth, and because WE are the ones who are experiencing the ascension process first for the benefit of all others, we are then entitled to create this New Earth exactly how we choose! So if you feel that you have suffered much through the ascension process, this is a just reward, so to speak! After a pure clean slate of the earth has been laid (reflecting its' original intention of a higher vibrating playground for experiencing and creating), and after we have become a more pure, clean human model again through all the purging and releasing we have done (much more about this can be found in the *Ascension Symptoms* chapter), we can then choose what we wish this New Earth to become. And it is entirely up to us. The ascension process has enabled us to release and spin off any influence or identity from our star families, and we are now free to create without any of their influence. Know as well, that many higher star beings are at our beckoned call if and when we need their wisdom and assistance.

A bit more regarding our star families of origin needs to be said here. Most of us actually go back even further than our incarnations through the stars. When January of 2006 arrived, we were able to connect very strongly to a much higher guidance system, as this is where we were now vibrating. All the archangels, spirit guides, ascended masters, and non-physical beings are actually simply manifestations and aspects of ourselves. We seem to be able to place more confidence and trust in outside sources, and love that drama! So after having the opportunity to leap ahead in January, the energy of our "star homes" was really gone. We were then vibrating and being a much higher energy that resonated with a much higher and more highly evolved aspect of ourselves. This aspect went very deep, was much more ancient, and created a much more frequent, easy and better aligned connection with a new guide or non-physical being at a much higher level...which was of course a higher aspect of ourselves! And as we progress through this on-going process, we will eventually evolve beyond the loving, non-physical beings that are watching over us now. We are all helping each other and we are all one.

I'm Knocking! Can I Come In Yet?

But there is yet more to this process of ascension. Yes, the ascension process involves a return to Source. Many souls have been around for eons of time. As mentioned before, they have infused their energy into many different realities and scenarios and experienced much. They have vibrated and expanded as high and as far as they can in this particular universe. Creation exists in a hierarchical form. We cannot go farther than we are currently vibrating. When we are communicating with non-physical beings, this is why they can come where we are, but we cannot go where they are until we are vibrating there or *being* their vibration. This is also why "channelers" vary so greatly with the information they present. One can only receive information for which they are a vibrating match for. Archangel Michael may have one message when speaking through one person and have an entirely different message when speaking through another. In all cases, whether through dimensional travel or through channeling, we cannot go higher than we are vibrating, but we *can* go lower......we just cannot stay at the lower vibrations for very long. It's much too dense and heavy.

As we progress through the ascension process, we are purifying. The more pure we become, the higher we begin to vibrate and through our human form, we are then able to access higher dimensions. This is why some of us are in one ascension reality or phase, and others are at another. The "first wavers" (of the lightworkers) are older in human chronological age and agreed to go first. These souls began their process of awakening a much longer time ago. They were a brave and strong group who began the first ripples of change on the planet. They had to break into tight and dense territory and begin to shake things up. They were also the first ones to experience the ascension process when it really began in earnest in 2000. When the time was right, their programming kicked in, and away they went. During this time, not nearly as much was known about ascension and it was difficult for these pioneers! Many did not know what in the world was happening to them at that time.

I have come to know from personal experience that we become activated when our programming kicks in and this creates a moving, breathing, and very real process. When the vibration of the planet reaches a certain point through the raising of the personal vibration (or consciousness) of its inhabitants as well as planetary vibration (the vibration of the physical planet herself), this will activate programming in individuals who are wired for this particular stage at this particular time. It is yet another situation of matching vibrations and the time varies for each individual according to their plan before birth. A particular frequency surrounding us that has just been reached is what creates the activation. It was all pre-planned. And through the ascension process the planetary frequency, as well as our individual frequencies are continually rising.

In 2001, I was nowhere near ready for my role as a pioneer and way show-er as I was not vibrating at this level. I had experienced a great amount of trauma and abuse in my life, and even though I had received many healings and worked very diligently on my personal growth for many years, I was still embodying a lot of damaged inner child energy. But my soul knew otherwise and had a plan. If I was going to be able to fulfill the role I had planned before birth, I had to be there. Thus, at my soul level, I created a crash course readiness scenario through a very minor auto accident. I crushed my right leg and this experience literally wiped away all the denser aspects of myself in one huge, intense, and vast sweep of a higher and very powerful hand. All that was left of me were the soles of my shoes. I don't recommend this way of arriving to anyone, as it proved to be very tumultuous, but I was very behind and needed to catch up.

So how then, do hierarchies come into play within the ascension process? One cannot go farther (or higher) than they are vibrating or *being*. When we reached critical mass in

August of 2005, this began a process of setting up and aligning for a New planet Earth. We had completed much of the purifying process and were now ready to begin creating a New World in the physical. Several phases were implemented which we needed to go through before the next big step in January of 2006. When January arrived, a big door slammed shut. Some were granted access while others were not. This was simply because access to anywhere cannot be granted until one is vibrating the same as that particular place. No judgment here, as this is simply a matter of energy and how it works. We cannot go higher than we are vibrating. We cannot arrive in the higher realms until we are *being* them. But we can go back to the old world or lower realms when we choose, but it feels so downright uncomfortable there that we cannot be there for very long. So during this time, many loved ones and individuals in our lives simply went somewhere else and there occurred a great separation of friends and family for some of us.

And yet there is a much more influential and powerful role of the hierarchies that involves the ascension process, and this one occurs at the higher levels. At higher or soul levels, many of us have reached the highest vibrating level of this particular universe. Our souls have gone far and expanded as much as they can. These souls have chosen as their last grand experience to participate in this awesome and spectacular plan of ascending as a group through the human body. This is their last hoorah. Through their last experience in this universe, they are ascending as a whole through human form and through this process they will enable all the angels, archangels, galactics, and higher non-physical beings of light to ascend (start over and anew) after they do.

Some of these souls now in human form will go on to become the New angels and stewards of the planet Earth and beyond in this universe. As all creation is composed of endless universes, all vibrating at different levels in a hierarchical order, other souls will finish their last hoorah here and go on to a very new universe. These particular souls are very complete with their experiences in this universe. They are now very ready to begin a very new experience in a very new universe. They will arrive in the next universe on the "bottom rung" and begin their journeys of expansion at their very next level of evolution. They will be allowed access so to speak, because they are now vibrating this higher vibration of the next universe. So if you are no longer craving any new information or reading any more books, you are probably done here and ready for some very new experiences indeed...experiences and knowledge that you have never encountered before. You may feel ancient here now and perhaps a bit cocky and very tired, but just wait until you arrive in a higher vibrating universe! You will most likely feel like a new and budding babe.

Most of these souls are now in the process of setting up and readying a very New planet Earth so that they will have left behind a New palette of creation. This is their legacy, so to speak. They are leaving this New palette behind so that other souls can utilize it as a playground for experiencing, creating, and evolving after they have departed.

Say That Again?

- Those of us currently residing on Earth chose to experience this Shift of the Ages (or ascension process) and therefore we knew somewhere in our consciousness that we were here for an unprecedented and monumental event.

- The ascension process involves a raising of our individual and planetary frequency, creating a higher level consciousness and more highly evolved planet that will eventually result in higher ways of being and living.
- We made our plans before we were born, so some agreed to go first to begin this evolutionary process and therefore guide and pave the way for others to follow (these are the first wavers and the lightworkers). This process began for them first, but as the ascension process bumps up exponentially, many are very rapidly experiencing the ascension process now.
- The year 2000 brought in the most intense phases of ascension as *we are dying while we are alive*. Like the 3D death process, we have to release every aspect of ourselves before we can "ascend" and begin again.
- Along with a repositioning of the planets in the universe, we decided as a group of souls to begin again and start over. Therefore, we came together from every part of the universe with representation from every star system and infused our energy into human form for this unprecedented event.
- By having all this representation now here on Earth for this Shift of the Ages, we are then able to bring back this experience of returning to Source through ourselves and then reverberate it to everything back "home", there-by capturing all of the universe.
- During this time, the Earth is being restored to its original blueprint where it will again be a playground for creation.
- This time, we will take creation further than the energies of Lemuria or Atlantis and be able to create

22

freely a very New planet Earth of our making and desires.

•   All the current angels, galactics, non-physical beings of light and every other existing entity in this universe will follow our path and ascend after we do. We are showing the way for all else to benefit from and follow.

•   As we continue with the ascension process of returning to Source, we will be vibrating higher and higher, so some will eventually become the New stewards or angels for the New planet Earth and beyond.

•   As all creation is orderly with specific hierarchies, others will complete their missions here after the New universe and New Earth are established. They will then move on into a brand New hierarchy of a much higher vibrating and different universe (another of endless universes) and begin again at the bottom rung.

•   These souls are leaving and completing their experiences in the current universe as they have done it all and gone as far as they can go here. They have chosen to leave an incredible New palette behind through their creations of a New and clean structure for all who follow to utilize and experience after they are gone.

•   The planet Earth is the template and jewel where it is all happening for the ascension process and Shift of the Ages.

So then, with this monumental process now underway, what contributes to all the power behind the throne?   What is pushing us along and how is it manifesting in our lives?

2

THE ENERGY SHIFTS

ON AUGUST 11, 1999 we experienced a solar eclipse and the beginning of the Grand Cross planetary alignment. The second Grand Cross occurred a few days later on August 17th. The second Grand Cross occurred twelve years to the day after the Harmonic Convergence of 1987, and 269 days (which is an exact human gestation period) before the Star of Jerusalem alignment of May 5, 2000 (dubbed the birth of the Age of Enlightenment). January 1, 2000 fell exactly on the midpoint between August 17, 1999 and May 5, 2000. Astrologers concurred that the occurrence of the Grand Cross in the fixed signs suggested a time of spiritual repositioning and preparing for an upward move.

The ascension process has been on-going for many years, but for our purposes here, I will be discussing energetic shifts from this point forward, as the year 2000 marked the beginning of a very accelerated time for ascension.

Also, directly after the Grand Cross alignment, most lightworkers had dreams that they were dying. Every lightworker I knew had a dying dream. This was because this time had been allocated as the end of the old world. These dreams of dying were a manifestation of another possible scenario that could have been played out. Lightworkers could have all left at this time and gone back home. But as we know, they stayed and the ascension process began.

For me, except for the Harmonic Convergence, experiencing the Grand Cross alignment was the first time I really felt a big shift with the energies. Knowing very little about astrology and astronomy (and I still don't!), I only knew that something was occurring because I could *feel* it. Like a big blast of the feminine arriving, I found myself in a different world and could clearly see how things really were at the higher levels behind the veil. During this time, I took three months off and disconnected from the outer world. I had no source of income, but knew I needed to be in this space and really take some time just for *me*. I learned so much during this time, as I was truly experiencing first hand the energies of the higher realms. And because I was in a higher vibration that arrived through this latest energy shift, all my needs were magically and miraculously met.

I remember needing a bowl one day. I had just recently arrived in Southwest Colorado from the mountains of North Carolina and had brought very few belongings with me. Just then, there was a knock on the door and there stood my neighbor with a bowl in her hands. She thought I might be needing it and had an extra one. Another day I was feeling hungry around mid-day and wishing I had some lunch. I was walking into a Wal-Mart and an employee approached me and offered me a free lunch, as they were demonstrating a new cooking grill. After awhile my rent eventually became due, and I miraculously found the exact amount needed lying on the seat of my car along with a bouquet of sage. This is how it was for me during this very special time of experiencing this new blueprint arriving through the Grand Cross alignment.

The peace I felt during these three months was indescribable. And the gratitude for the simplest of things was profound. Just walking along a country road and seeing the beauty of nature and a herd of sheep walking along with me would bring me to tears. As I continually had all my needs met, this left much more time in my life as I did not need to extend any energies trying to make things happen. What was left then, as I discovered, was time for simply creating and being. Extending myself in any way felt grossly off, and I was unable to do it. Appreciating music and the arts was another great pleasure I discovered at an even higher level. It was a truly special time for me, and after my three months, the energies began to wane and I found myself returning to the outside world and a much lower vibrating reality.

What had actually occurred here? What was going on?

The New (Or Old) Templates Arrive

Throughout the ascension process, we are continually receiving new (or higher vibrating) energetic blueprints or templates. And they are arriving in different ways. Like the blueprint of Lemuria, some arrive from within the earth as they are basically unveiled when the vibrational frequencies of the planet reach a certain level, while others arrive from the cosmos. This is an on-going pattern and will continue. As everything above and below is in on the ascension experience and all working together as a team, these energy shifts arriving from the sky are very key components of the process. The Grand Cross alignment, then, brought in a blueprint for a higher realms reality, but it will take several years before the entire earth will be in alignment and manifesting this New blueprint and way of belng.

"What *really* is an energy shift?" you may be wondering.

In June of 2002, I was visiting Southwest Colorado during a time of great fires. It seemed that a large part of Arizona, New Mexico, Utah, and Colorado were all burning at once, with many substantial fires blazing at record levels and even merging together. During this time, I began to feel a great amount of energy moving through me...to the point that my body began to interpret it as panic and anxiety. So much energy began to move through my body that my toenails actually fell off!

Part of ascension involves a great purging within and without of old lower, darker and denser energies that no longer match the raising vibration of ourselves and the planet. In order to accommodate more light and become closer to and more of Source, we need to empty out in order to make room for this more highly vibrating energy to embody us. The planet is purifying through fire, water, earthquakes, and wind, etc., along with a purification of our human selves through letting go of Illusions and misperceptions, defense mechanisms and behaviors, and especially the ego. During this time, Southwest Colorado was reacting to an energy shift, and I was reacting to it as well.

When we experience an energy shift, much changes and begins to move. Around the year 2000, the shifts began as a very *pushing* kind of energy. They created very strong feelings of tension, stress, and feeling overwhelmed along with other reactions too numerous to discuss in this section. Because we were not yet wired and vibrating highly as human beings, many of the first wavers *really* felt these first shifts in energy. For others, it was not yet time for their ascension process and they felt absolutely nothing. For me, I could barely accommodate them after awhile. I got to where I would literally break into tears when I knew one was coming, as I felt them so intensely. They greatly affected my life to a degree that was nearly incapacitating. So much energy would move through my body that I would lIterally shake, begin hyperventilating, could not think, and would almost go into shock. And there were a few times when I actually did go into shock. My heart really took a beating also as it could not accommodate this influx of energy. Eventually I took a stand and declared that I would not be willing to participate and would have no problem leaving the planet if this was how it was going to be. In addition, as our bodies begin to acclimate and vibrate higher, we feel these shifts less and less. So after my stand and some acclimation, I was then able to more easily assimilate the New energies.

What is creating these shifts?

We are receiving blasts of higher energy from the sun. I really do not know much about the scientific angle to ascension (and there most certainly is a scientific explanation as well). As mentioned before, at higher levels, we decided as a group of souls to raise our consciousness through one great big whoosh (and as a whole) instead of through gradual incarnations, and thus began a summoning. And again, as the planets began a repositioning in the cosmos, along with our summoning as human beings, the process began. But there is a pattern and orderly fashion to these shifts.

Getting To Know The Shifts

On June 8, 2004, we experienced the Venus Transit. This particular astrological occurrence brought in the arrival of the feminine and the energy of love. I will use the Venus Transit as an example of how the energy shifts that arrive through the planets work to support and create our ascension process.

Each energy shift contains a blueprint or what I call an earmark of a particular theme or energy. Some planetary alignments bring in substantial shifts, while at other times we experience more minor shifts. None-the-less, the shifts are always on-going and arrive closer and closer together as we progress through this process of raising our vibration personally and planetarily. It reminds me of the labor pains of birth as they begin slowly and then intensify while they come at closer and closer intervals. And the higher we vibrate and the more we progress, the more magnified everything becomes.

So in comes a very strong energy of the feminine and of love through the Venus Transit. The feminine and love are what Venus is all about. Venus, then, was the perfect carrier or vessel to support this energy. All the planets have their own specific vibration and purpose (remember how each planet vibrated uniquely for all the individuals during the soul readings?). The planets, just like our Mother Earth, are living, breathing entities in themselves with their own personalities. The advent of the arrival of this energy brought through the "container" of Venus (who was very excited, by the way, to be contributing its' special purpose), affected every existing thing. Everything was affected according to how it related to this energy. When a New energy arrives, every living thing will find itself aligning to it. If you are out of whack and not vibrating in this newly arriving higher way you will need to adjust...and basically everyone needs to adjust!   And this is where the ascension symptoms come into play as well.   These symptoms are a manifestation of the adjustments and alignments we are making that are enabling us to vibrate higher and higher.

But there is another continual pattern that occurs when these shifts arrive.   First we feel the New energy.   Being that this energy is of a much higher way and vibration, it feels wonderful when it arrives.   It clearly shows us what the higher way of this particular blueprint looks and feels like.   We are then able to tap into it later on as we have now connected to it.   It is now a part of our being and our New and higher vibrating reality.   But before we are able to make it a continual reality and way of being, we have to go through the alignment process.

So we go from a place of feeling exuberant and ecstatic "Now we have finally arrived"!   Then an immense letdown as we progress into the aligning stage.   We may even think that someone is playing a big trick on us and dangling a forever on-going carrot in front of our noses!   During the aligning stage, the very polar opposite of the earmark of the newly arriving energy arrives right on its' heels.   We go from feeling wonderful while we experience the upside of this particular theme of this energy, to really feeling the pendulum swing and experiencing the darker and lower aspects of this energy. What is happening here is the integration of the polarity.   All must be encompassed and integrated, because in the higher realms there is no polarity.   For example, if the newly arriving energy has a theme of *acceptance*, we will then experience directly following it an energy of *rejection*.   And being that we are so upside down while in the process of turning rightside up, the integration process is considerably longer in duration than the experiences of being in the higher forms of this newly arriving energy.

This is how the planets create shifts for us, but we also experience shifts when solar flares are occurring. The solar flares are different in that they specifically bring in very strong blasts of higher crystalline energy. Crystalline energy is the New structure or the New blueprint that we are evolving into. It is what we will be made of...it is the New fiber of our being. These strong blasts or surges are what can create anxiety and tension, heart palpitations, severe bloating and indigestion, etc. and for some, make their toenails fall off!

As soon as a particular energy shift is integrated, we then begin another. And in between, there is yet another phenomenon occurring.

I Feel Blahhhh...

In order to fill up with more of our true selves (or with Source), we must first empty out. I liken it to a tank being drained before it can fill up again. We would not want to fill something up on top of old energy or any kind of death or decaying energy. Old energy first needs to depart. Moving out old and denser energy is occurring through the shifts as they serve to push out what cannot exist in the higher realms.   But there also occur times of great emptiness. After a time of substantial movement, we usually experience a great void or lag in the energies.

This regular occurring phase manifests at all levels. At lower levels, the biggest *feeling* and experience of the emptiness relates to having no support. Everything may seem to be pulling out or *taking* from us instead of giving or filling us up.

During these times we usually experience a big wane in our finances. Nothing seems to go right and manifesting is at an all time low. We may feel very disconnected and removed from everyone and everything. The energetic tide is out. We are deflated.

This phase is a regular part of the ascension process and one of my least favorites, but it always passes. "The emptiness" can last as long as it needs to. During substantial shifts, its' duration is determined by the critical mass. You may be quite done emptying out and integrating for this round, but not everyone else is and this creates a waiting period. This can be difficult as well, but know we are all in this together supporting our brothers and sisters as we contribute to the whole.

The longer in duration the wane or emptiness period is, the bigger the next arriving shift will be. When we have a very long period of emptiness, it is because we are getting ready to experience a very New and higher way of being. We simply need to have enough room within us to embody what is to come. It is almost as if the tide has gone way, way out so that it can build before it arrives in full force again...almost like a tsunami. The more that goes out, the more that comes in.

During the emptiness phase, much is being recalibrated at all levels. This is part of the realigning process. We cannot move forward again until everything at all levels is in place and ready to go. It is during this time that we may feel passionless, lethargic, apathetic, depressed, and very tired. We are simply rebooting and realigning for the next round. We cannot get into our new bed until it is made.

During these times of emptiness, another necessary by-product occurs as well. We have the opportunity to become very clear about where we want to go and who we want to be. The emptiness can create disappointment and feelings of let down as we are not feeling any support. Feeling deflated and depressed are common experiences. If you allow it, this can create a wonderful opportunity to really see what is working for you in your life and what is not. Being disappointed, angry, and frustrated can fuel blame, but in a good way. It can make clear what needs to stay and what needs to go, and what you have had enough of. This is a perfect by-product of this phase, as you would not want to move forward (when the energy returns again) into something that really no longer fits you.

This is part of the recalibrating phase at the lower levels. At the higher levels, everything is being moved into place for the arrival of another surge and phase of higher-level being. Manifesting begins again with ease and rapidity and we are in a very New space indeed. Basically speaking, the more we empty out and the longer it lasts, the more we will receive and the higher our surrounding reality will be vibrating when the energies return. During the emptiness stage, we are simply feeling and experiencing the results of being "unplugged" and "in between".

Harmonizing With The Gift Of The Planets

Not only do the planets bring in New blueprints with the arrival of unusual and more sparsely occurring alignments, but their continual presence is supporting us in other ways as well.

You're moving along happily in your life and suddenly you hear that it is time for Mercury to go retrograde. "Not again!" you may exclaim. "Didn't we just go through a Mercury retrograde?!" We often hear of the things we should not do during a Mercury retrograde and may even feel as if we are on hold until this planetary phase is over. But Mercury turning retrograde brings us many gifts and special opportunities as well.

March of 2006 was a very tumultuous and active month regarding the cosmos. We had just reached critical mass in August of 2005, had a big *crossing over* experience in January of 2006, and then began a massive physical detoxing in February in order to align ourselves with our new higher vibrating surroundings. Then in March, we experienced a lunar eclipse, a solar eclipse, and an equinox. Also, for the majority of the month, Mercury was in retrograde.

What a wild ride it was and the celestial bodies were supporting our progress all the way. The lunar eclipse occurred first and created an energetic environment that activated within us an opportunity to go inward and deeper, connecting with our shadow sides. After the eclipse, we could then start anew with a greater awareness. Next occurred the equinox, bringing in a new beginning with a "balanced scale" so to speak. New pieces to support our new creations were emerging and being supported through these energies. And then at the end of the month occurred a solar eclipse. The solar eclipse again supported a new beginning. The sun was covered and again emerged bringing in a whole new day and the beginning of a new year.

During this time, there were also other on-going intermittent energetic occurrences as well. The month of March experienced several brief energy surges not relating to any celestial bodies. These surges served to lift up the planet and ourselves in vibration. Like big blasts of higher vibrating energy, we were catapulted from our grooves and elevated to even higher levels. The surges served to create the "rungs" of our new palette of foundation for this new reality of 2006. These surges would be on-going until the equinox in June. Like big blasts of intense energy hitting the planet, these surges knocked us out of our old grooves, catapulted us higher, and for the sensitive, even created a sense of being traumatized.

For almost the entire month of March, Mercury was retrograde. With critical mass having been reached, creating a new world had begun. Were we ready? Not exactly, but the vibration and blueprint of each of these celestial bodies along with the energy surges were greatly supporting our progress. And Mercury being retrograde was a key component. Mercury allowed us to *go back* and really re-examine what we wanted for ourselves. It supported us in finishing anything that had been left undone, therefore freeing us up to move forward when the energies again arrived to support our forward progress through the solar eclipse and the equinox. And around the time of the eclipse and the equinox, Mercury would again begin its' forward movement. All in perfect order and with perfect divine timing.

(As I write these words, it is March 2006 and we are in a Mercury retrograde. I knew I would be writing an ascension manual, but the ascension manual energy and experience was very old for me. Although it is always on-going, I had gone through much of my process a few years before and did not want to dive into it again. For me, it was long gone. But along came the retrograde, and along with other situations being completed in my life, it was a perfect time to write this book. This planetary activity was allowing me to be in the flow of *going back*. Mercury was indeed supporting me during this perfect time to write the *Ascension Primer*.)

This year of 2006 was a very pivotal year. Before we could create the new, we had to prepare. The first half of the year supported us in every way to become aligned for the New, so that in the second half we would be vibrating in alignment and perfectly matched for the arrival of the New in form. We cannot pile up new energy upon old energy. And we also needed to be clear about what it really was that we wanted to create. In order to create anything, one has to first *be* it...and the events of March were supporting this probability in a perfect and miraculous way.

When we become aware of and harmonize with the gifts that the planets offer us, our journey can be much smoother. At higher levels, everything in form is going in the same direction and supporting our ascension process of expanding and moving into a reality of higher consciousness...even though it may not appear to be the case.

Say That Again?

- Energy shifts are on-going and greatly contribute to our evolutionary ascension process.
- The energy shifts serve to bring in a higher level vibration which we then connect to, enabling us to eventually create and *be* New templates for a higher vibrating reality and higher vibrating human.
- There are several forms of energy shifts:
  - Some arrive as unusual and intermittent (but powerful and perfectly planned) planetary alignments.
  - Some emerge from beneath the earth when the planet reaches a distinct and higher frequency. These energies have been secretly

buried for eons of time just waiting for this incredible time to be unveiled and to re-emerge.

o   The sun also sends us blasts of crystalline energy in the form of solar flares. These energy surges greatly "push" the older and denser energies out. They also bring in the New crystalline blueprints or "glue" that form our New make-up and create our New internal foundation.   This form of energy shift is the most forceful, dramatic and powerful and creates the most immediate change.

•   All newly arriving energy first brings in a new blueprint of higher vibrating and more evolved energy that feels great. What immediately follows is a time of integration and alignment that does not feel so great.

•   After we are done integrating and aligning, we usually experience a phase of emptiness or of feeling lifeless. We are simply rebooting our systems to ready ourselves for more forward movement.

•   The planets and celestial bodies and events that occur through them on a regular basis are supporting us as well, and it can greatly help to align ourselves with the gifts of the energy they bring.

There is a higher plan being implemented that certainly supports our ascension process and harmonizing and working together as a team is part of this plan. There is so much love and support for us at the higher levels.   And even what appears to be darkness is on our side as well.

3

THE PROCESS

ONE OF MY GREAT loves and favorite creative outlets is creating practical fabric art in the form of upholstery, window treatments, and pillows as well as refinishing furniture. Right now I am changing the color scheme in my home. I am going to a teal color with shades of sage green to create an ancient southwestern theme. In between writing the sections of this book, I will jump up and work on my latest furniture project. I am distressing a bookcase in this color scheme to create a rustic look. First I painted three layers in the color shades I just mentioned. Now I am in the process of sanding away the colors I just painted to reveal the shades underneath, as well as the unfinished wood itself. First I created very new colors on top of the original wood and now I am undoing what I painted. And this is the same with the ascension process. We are most certainly *undoing*.

Like the original wood underneath, our souls are the basic foundation of our existence. As we incarnated and infused our energies in many different places and in many different forms, we then, like the different colors of paint, added additional energies to our original soul energy. And these additional energies were not as pure as our very original soul energy as they became skewed from the experiences we had encountered. The ascension process involves sanding away, or letting go and releasing all the additional energies that we had piled on top of our original soul energy.

Through this process we find ourselves letting go, letting go, and then letting go again. It seems to never end. And as human beings, our sense of security is challenged over and over through this process. But as we progress and continue with our journey of returning to Source, we eventually find a New security, and that security is Source itself and our true selves. We think we cannot go any further or stretch anymore, but the process continues and we find that through these immense challenges, we really can do it. And in addition, after each phase is complete, we are stronger and better than ever before.

Letting go and undoing come in many forms through the ascension process, and many of them have surprised us.

Letting Go Through Intolerance And Apathy

One thing I have said over and over for several years is that *the higher realms are not what you might think*. Much of what we have been taught or read about is highly inaccurate. Although this is not a simple process, basically it all boils down to simplicity and how energy responds and interacts with itself. There are higher and lower forms of vibrating energy creating things that feel good and things that do not. So then, there is no meaning to anything. Meaning is simply what we choose to place on any particular manifestation. Some things may feel good to one person according to how they interpret them, and may feel very unpleasant to another. A rule of thumb, then, might be that things either feel good or they feel bad. It's that simple.

As we begin to vibrate higher and higher we become less and less of a match to what has been created so far on this planet and also to any lower vibrating aspects of other human behaviors and realities. One might think that as we become more spiritual we embody a great compassion, understanding, and tolerance at higher levels than we ever have before. But this is not the case. As we progress through ascension and begin to vibrate higher and higher, we find ourselves becoming highly intolerant of any lower vibrating energies. We simply cannot be in their presence for very long and we may even become angry and frustrated with them as well.

There is a method to this madness. As mentioned in earlier sections of this book, there is a hierarchy to energetic levels and dimensions. When we reach higher realities, it is very difficult to reside or spend time in the lower realities. We are simply not a match to them anymore. This response also has other benefits. The intolerance greatly encourages us to create more on the outside that matches how we are vibrating, feeling and *being* on the inside. If our outside reality feels downright awful, we will most assuredly be inspired to save ourselves through our need to feel better by creating higher ways of living and being. And by not tolerating and refusing to be a part of the old reality, as we literally cannot stomach it anymore, it makes us literally refuse to participate, therefore withdrawing any energy of support. If we do not become involved in something and negate it, it cannot survive because there is no energy to make it real and alive. It will simply cease to be as it will not be residing in anyone's consciousness.

Through this intolerance we are also being very direct. As we progress into higher vibrating human beings, we find that we can no longer beat around the bush, sit by and watch, or take a long winding road to get anywhere. Higher energy moves in a straight shot. It does not go here and there, make excuses and support friends and family even though they are in unhealthy situations, or sit blindly by. It is simple and direct. No wishy washy uncertainty and passivity. The time is up for tolerating the old and for waiting. It's the higher way or no way. At some level we know this, and at times can find ourselves addressing the lower vibrations very directly. In this way, this is a higher form of love. It involves an inability to support the lower vibrations in anything. We are actually being supportive and loving in that we are now supporting the highest ways through this intolerance. We are actually being spiritual warriors of higher truth and greatly helping others.

In the higher realms we create through a partnership with Source and as we are becoming more and more of Source ourselves, we must connect much more deeply now in order to create the higher ways. During these years of ascension, it can appear that we are getting absolutely nowhere. It may seem that nothing ever goes our way or that we are receiving very little support for getting what we want.

This is really not the case. We do not want to create things that are not of a higher vibration or that will no longer fit in the near future. In other ways, we cannot create from ego in the higher realms. When we are not getting what we want, it is usually because we won't be in that situation or reality very soon, or that we are not yet ready. If there is something that you really feel you *must* have, then you are not ready to receive it. It is ironic that we always get what we want when we no longer want it. What is happening here is that we have lost our attachment, which places us in a position for perfect creating. In addition, we are not then, creating from our ego. This is all part of the ascension process.

Through it all, we can get pretty discouraged at times. When we get discouraged and let down over and over again, and feel that all our dreams have shattered, we become apathetic. This is perfect. It puts us into a space of letting go. We simply do not care anymore. This makes us let go and release the energy of attachment. We are then residing in neutral energy with no agendas and this allows much more of Source to enter. And of course, allows us to let go of many of the illusions.

Letting Go Through The Gift Of Darkness

At the highest levels, we are all going in the same direction to assist in this miraculous ascension process. Everyone and everything is in on this together and working as a team. At the highest levels, everything always goes in the same direction, supporting and assisting each soul with great love and with a mutual consensus of the same desire and purpose. There is so much love at the higher levels because all experiences are created from a perfect synchronization of harmonizing energies.

Just as the planets are vibrating with us as we are all one, all souls are united as one as well. In my book **Remembering Your Soul Purpose / A Part Of Ascension**, I devote an entire chapter to this scenario. It explains how it relates to our parents or primary caretakers, as it is so relevant to the process of creation. This scenario also relates to all souls in other ways too. Our parents or primary caretakers had relationships with us that many might interpret as abusive. To sidetrack a bit here, nearly all lightworkers were born into abuse. This was certainly part of the grand plan as we knew before we were born that we would use these relationships and what they offered us as an opportunity to transmute the lower vibrating energies or the darkness. We gladly took on these darker energies as we knew how powerful we were as souls and knew, then, that we would certainly succeed. This was a part of the plan that we devised in order to assist in raising the frequency of the planet as a whole.

But there is also another reason we chose to experience the darkness through abuse. Darkness always serves to spur us on by giving us the contrast we need to search for something higher and better and to create something New. Darkness is the power or fuel that ignites the light. If you had a parent that was very absent, for instance, it would create in you a strong desire for unity, and thus support your soul purpose of creating unity. A parent that continually expressed to you that you were nothing, would spur you on to show the world that you were really something. These parental relationships were planned at higher levels to specifically create the traits that you came to embody. The souls of these abusive parents loved you so much they that agreed to provide the necessary interactions to support you in your purpose.

In November of 2004, George W. Bush was re-elected as president here in the United States where I reside. Many lightworkers as well as many other citizens of the US were absolutely devastated. They felt that this man was leading the country astray and promoting many dark and horrific acts as well as making decisions that were not of the highest vibration. He was, to them, embodying the worst case scenario that we could ever imagine. Lightworkers felt a great sense of disbelief and devastation and sank to very low depths of futility. What they failed to see was that everything was in divine right order.

This beautiful soul, George W. Bush, had agreed to provide the contrast needed to wake up as many individuals as possible so that change could be created. Not enough people on the planet were ready and willing to make change. It seems that things need to get really bad before people are willing to let go and finally embrace something New. George Bush provided the means to create the contrast needed so enough individuals would finally wake up. This amazing and divine soul has been waving a red flag for awhile now, trying to get everyone's attention so that there will no longer be apathy. He is giving people the opportunity to say "We don't want this anymore!" and to be able to more clearly define what it is that they *do* want. As darkness usually does, it is illuminating the opposite of the light so that individuals can get really clear regarding what the higher road really is.

Part of the ascension process involves a willingness to let go. Darkness can create the impetus to convince people to let go of the old and try something New. Darkness makes us ready to let go of the lower vibrations by making them *very dark*. It seems that things have to get pretty bad before enough people are ready to give up their securities and embrace change. And in addition, the darkness will continue for as long as it takes in order for a critical mass to be reached. So for those who have been ready for awhile (i.e. have let go of much and moved on into a higher way of being), it can be challenging to have to remain in uncomfortable outside manifestations of the collective until enough people wake up and are ready and willing to do something different. In other words, you may be ready to create a Newer and higher vibrating reality that matches the New you, but the collective, or majority of the planet, is not. This is when it can become challenging as the contrast of the outside world can feel downright awful and uncomfortable. So then, the darkness creates the impetus to let go of the old (as it is dark). It then takes enough individuals, or a critical mass who have let go of the old, denser energies, before the New can be created. Enough individuals though a critical mass are needed to create something New as the New needs to be embraced, wanted and needed. When the scales tip, then the New is ready to arrive through an opening of willingness and summoning from the critical mass. In this way, the darkness is supporting the process and contributing its' purpose in a beautiful and loving way.

Many lightworkers also feel that it is time that we have political representation that vibrates much higher. This cannot possibly happen now. The manifestation of a highly vibrating government and its representatives can only occur when it matches the vibration of the critical mass or enough of the collective. We are not there yet. For instance, it would not make sense for a being of light to be president of the United States right now, because not enough citizens could even relate to what this individual was about. There would be no matching of energies. He/she would not be representing the majority. To manifest something, one must first *be* it. The United States is not yet *being* a higher vibration as a whole. This process is gradual and involves huge change, and it cannot happen overnight. Even though many lightworkers think they are of a higher way, many are simply not. The higher way is simply in their mental processes and in their awareness. Their transmuting process, although intense and substantial, is not yet done. They are not yet *being* or vibrating what it is they desire a political leader to be. And once they *are* being it, they will no longer have the desire to have it manifest on the outside anyway.

In the higher realms, we do not create through contrast or polarity (or darkness). As we integrate the polarity more and more, and as we *become* the higher realms more and more, this form of creating will eventually cease to exist. Being that there is no dark or light, good or bad, or right or wrong, as we are all one, the higher realms does not look like this linear state of existence. Everything simply *is*.

The Dark Night Of The Soul

Another manifestation of darkness occurs when we are letting go of parts of our ego through a dark night of the soul. Several years ago I experienced a huge and intense leap in vibration. Being that I was so behind with being ready for what my soul came to contribute at this time, I needed to catch up and therefore, had a few intense crash courses of the ascension experience.

This particular time, I experienced a mirage of wild and bizarre symptoms that lasted several weeks, but all the strange symptoms had a meaning and purpose. At this time not much was known about ascension, so I had no idea what was really going on within me. I would lay my head down on the pillow at night and immediately begin to experience intense and rapid flashbacks, with frames and images flying past as I was releasing much from my past. They were so rapid and intense that I had to ask for a break! It was like a wild nightmare with such an extreme rapid and intense energy that I could barely tolerate it. I even began to feel traumatized. So much began occurring in my sleep that for awhile I began to dread going to sleep. But the most difficult part was the feeling of the darkness. During the daylight hours, I felt as though I had sunk to the depths of hell and could not for the life of me see a glimmer of light. The anguish I experienced cannot be described. My mother was visiting at the time and said that I looked as though I was having nightmares in the daytime. Thank goodness it only lasted a few weeks.

At certain levels, some would say that when our light begins to shine brighter, we immediately and automatically become attacked by the dark forces. The dark forces do not want more light to arrive and try to prevent it at all costs. I remember talking to a healer friend of mine on the phone during that time. She asked me to look and see where this darkness was coming from. Being fairly psychic, I could easily see a very dark and sinister being choreographing things behind the scenes. Then I felt even more darkness! Many psychics at the Association for Research and Enlightenment (A.R.E.) in Virginia Beach, Virginia (the Edgar Cayce organization where I once went for some psychic training), shared that when we begin to really open, it is a common occurrence to experience great attacks by the darkness. And when we experience the energy shifts on the planet, enabling us to receive much more light, they are always followed by the darkness. Some may say that it is the darkness or even the shadow government that is revving up again and pulling out even bigger guns so that the light will not succeed.

But none of this is an accurate explanation.

At higher levels, it is very easy to see that any darkness is simply an aspect of ourselves. At this time, I was releasing great amounts of lower vibrating energy that were within me. Humans love drama and seem to greatly enjoy placing an overstated meaning on energy. We seem to need a story in order to make sense of things. Very simply, when light arrives, darkness always does as well.

A common pattern with ascension reminds me of ships passing in the night. We may feel great waves of darkness, but during this time we may also experience heightened states of creativity and newly arriving light. As we go to higher levels, we can very easily feel the darkness we are in because it is up and departing. As we progress through the ascension process, the balance changes and we eventually begin to feel very little darkness and much more light. I can personally attest that this is the case! It gets much better...I promise!

Lower vibrating energy cannot exist in the same space as higher vibrating energy. This is why it moves out or transmutes when the light arrives. Like energy always attracts similar vibrating energy. When we let go of much of our ego, or rather denser energy that is not really connected to Source, all we may see is darkness because that is the current filter we are looking through.

When big energy surges arrive to support our raising consciousness, our egos can become terrified. Panic and anxiety can ensue. During my deepest ascension experience, I was living in one big, long panic attack that never ended. It was like a huge wave of terror, but I am wired highly sensitive, open, and psychic, so this was my experience. I eventually got to a point where I could observe from the outside and not take things personally. And acupuncture really helped during this time as well. It told my body that everything was really OK and my mind followed along. There is much more about the ascension symptoms and some tools for comfort in the chapters that follow.

Letting Go Through Exhaustion

One night I tuned into the *Dog Whisperer* on the National Geographic channel on television. Cesar Millan, an amazing man who works with dogs and can almost immediately create a healthy situation for a dog and its' owner, was working with an unusually troubled dog. This dog was attacking everyone and everything and was unpleasant for most anyone to be around. Being a more severe case than normal, Cesar decided to take this dog to his center and work with him there. This dog was aggressive and insecure and therefore it was near impossible for Cesar to connect with him. The dog's ego was protecting him in a very all-encompassing way. But Cesar knew exactly what to do. He put the dog on a treadmill and allowed him to run until he became very exhausted. He did this numerous times. In this state of exhaustion, the dog was much too tired to fight and therefore was able to get out of the way. He was then much more receptive to Cesar connecting with him and showing him a new and different experience. Ultimately, this dog fully integrated and became one with all the other dogs at the center. He had learned how to get out of his own way through the process of exhaustion. And this is what ascension does for us as well.

Like a diamond in the rough, we are being worn away over and over again. We may feel as though wave after wave is crashing down upon us and beating us up until there is nothing left. The ascension process makes us very weary and puts us in a state of not caring much about anything anymore. And this is perfect for two reasons. This process was really perfectly planned with perfect outcomes. Just like the dog in the Dog Whisperer story, when we become exhausted, we then get out of our own way. This allows us to be in a state of allowing and receiving. Being worn away, not caring anymore, and feeling exhausted is simply another way that the ascension process allows and supports us in letting go of more of our ego. Source can then enter when we no longer stand at the door and block it from opening. In addition, this process stops us from adhering to the ego parts of ourselves that think they know everything and insist on running the show. There is more room within us, then, to connect ever more fully with Source and our true selves. Just like the dog, we can then connect to experiences and knowledge that we may have never allowed ourselves to connect with before. And through this process, we also learn how to create from Source instead of through our egos.

Letting Go Through The Energy Shifts

When we begin to reach higher states of consciousness and to vibrate higher, the veil becomes thinner and thinner. In addition, as like energies always attract and connect with like energies, many changes and abrupt departures can occur for us.

Part of the ascension process involves our bloodlines and human families of origin. It has been a common occurrence for many of us lately to find ourselves at a family reunion, even though we may have not even seen our families for quite some time. What is happening here is a re-structuring or a re-calibrating of the bloodlines. Our families or primary caretakers were here to instill within us the traits we needed in order to support our purposes and roles for this experience on Earth. This is no longer necessary. What is needed now is an embodiment of the higher forms of our family traits, gifts, and talents without the contrast or darker aspects. We are re-uniting in order to let go and move forward in a New way.

There will come a time when you are vibrating higher and can therefore see things as they truly are. With the veil thinning more and more, we are then able to see our parents, relatives, and loved ones for who they truly are, without the cords that have bound us together through matching vibrations. In other words, the relationships we have had in the past are no longer necessary. We have evolved into higher beings and no longer need these connections. We can then clearly see what these individuals are about, know that they have absolutely nothing to do with us, and then let go of them. Our purposes and roles together are now complete and over. Many times we then part ways. If there is much love between us, we can stay connected, but this connection comes from no attachments or corresponding unbalanced energies. Because of this phenomenon, many of us are losing family and friends left and right. We are simply no longer a match. But as things progress, we will soon be matched with better fitting people, places, and roles. We are basically reincarnating into a New life and starting over with New roles and purposes as we are, most certainly, New people arriving in a New reality. The energy shifts are usually the precursor to these dramatic releases of jobs, people, and places. They serve to jolt us out of our old grooves and into New and better fitting grooves.

Letting Go Through A Health Crisis

In August of 2001, I was a passenger in a truck that was involved in a minor car accident. As a result of this accident, my right leg was shattered. The doctors were quite baffled as to how I could have sustained so much damage considering the nature of the circumstances. But all was in order, as I needed to be affected for a very long time in order to really cement in some new ways of being...ways where I had been really out of balance.

I needed physical therapy for two years, was on crutches for nine months, and had continual pain for a very long time. My pattern in the past was to flee when anything got unbearable or appeared that it might get unbearable. After the accident and the surgery, I could not go anywhere. I was forced to *go through* this process...no escaping.

Having experienced several rapes and molestations as a toddler and in childhood, feeling helpless and defenseless while unable to walk, run or flee because of a broken leg was simply terrifying. I felt overwhelmingly vulnerable. I did not believe I would survive this process. Even now while writing these words I am nearly brought to tears. I can't tell you all the issues and circumstances that were brought to the surface from this situation. I was forced to face them head-on. I cried rivers, had panic attacks and literally freaked out. It appeared that all the healings in the world had not made a dent for me. I had to experience this in a very real way in order to let go of so much.

I could not take care of myself and had to learn to get out of the way and receive. My power, or what I thought was my power, was gone. Being used to spending much of my time "up there" and not down here was no longer possible. Unable to move much or walk, I was forced into learning what it was like to be grounded. I had to be "here" in this place that had always been so uncomfortable. Several days before the accident, my big, beautiful non-physical companion had appeared and told me that something very unpleasant was about to occur. And while on the gurney awaiting surgery, my non-physical soul group appeared and told me that I would not be the same after the surgery...and boy, were they right!

So much of my ego was swept away. I did not know who I was anymore. I was gone. And those who visited me while I was in the hospital said I had never looked more beautiful. I was dying and looked awful. How could they say these things? I assumed they were just being polite. As I have now come to know, what they were seeing was the original innocence. And this is what was left of me.

Many of us have had "the health crisis" as it serves to assist with ascension in so many ways, all arriving through one experience. It forces us to get out of our own way. It forces us to let go of the ego parts that we will not be needing in the higher realms and these parts most certainly do not know what they are doing. And feeling vulnerable and defenseless is a very common occurrence with ascension, as our ego defense mechanisms are now gone but the outside world is still "dangerous".

The health crisis will last as long as it needs to until we adopt new methods of being…it will last until we are realigned. If it was of short duration, it would not have the impact necessary to change us through integrating new habits and ways. It shakes us up because it is supposed to. And for each of us, our own individual health crisis will fit us to a tee. It was designed to affect us precisely in the ways that are needed for our own individual and unique changes.

What Happened To My "Job"?

There comes a time for many when working a regular job is no longer possible. Many times it may not even be your idea. You may find yourself suddenly getting laid off, you may have a health situation that prohibits you from becoming involved in your regular form of employment, you may relocate to a new geographical area, or you simply may find that you just cannot go to your job for one more day.

If you are one that is very responsible and feels a need to be supporting yourself through outside employment, this newly arriving situation may come as a shock to you. When it is time, it is time. Your soul knows what it is doing. When it is time to end your old role and a major part of your old life, it will simply just happen. You can look for a job all you want, but you will never get one. You are simply not supposed to be working in this way anymore and that is that. Done.

"I'm not being supported by the universe anymore!" you may cry. "How am I supposed to live with no money and no job?!" you may declare. In actuality, you *are* being supported by the universe. You are being realigned to a new way of being that involves much less ego and much more of who you really are. And in addition, during severe periods of the ascension process when your symptoms prohibit you from functioning, you cannot work anyway.

All in all, this is the time when miracles occur. After the Grand Cross alignment in 2000, I could not get a job anywhere. A close friend of mine was totally baffled. I had a longstanding pattern of getting every job I wanted right off the bat. This time no one would hire me. I finally gave up. So I then decided to go into my creativity and start something from there. Being used to working for non-profits for most of my life and saving everyone and everything, this was quite a change to be actually doing something for *me*. But I found a pattern here. When I put myself first, everything flowed and absolutely fell into my lap. Otherwise, things would simply short circuit and go nowhere...as well as feeling downright awful.

And then a year later I had the accident. Again, my old and very responsible self wanted to jump right into non-profit consulting and grant writing while on crutches, putting my newly discovered creativity phase behind me. But a big booming voice and my intuition said very strongly that I would never work again. Period. I would not work again because from then on I would be "joying" instead of "working". I haven't worked a day since 2000. And I have never been lacking for financial support.

In the higher realms we live by being in our passion and in our creativity. Nothing is ever done for "the money". Decisions are not made according to monetary considerations. They are made according to what makes us come alive and feel great, even if they don't make any practical or logical sense. At soul levels, we find that we are totally supported when we place ourselves into this way of being. After I broke my leg and realized that I would no longer work at an outside job, someone gave me $10,000. I needed to make my declaration first though, as the universe always follows our lead. "Oh! So this is what we are doing!" the universe says. We set the pace and the universe follows along. After I was able to get off of my crutches, I went through a wonderful phase where I took every kind of class relating to creativity that I could. It was divine. It was all about *me*.

And then I went through another massive phase of ascension leaping and could barely function. All during this time, I was supported financially. I was where I needed to be and this was what was most important. From then on, I have stayed in my passion and in creative outlets that feel like utter joy and fun all the time. It is a wonderful life indeed, but I would not be here if I hadn't been willing to let go of my inappropriate sense of *responsibility* from the old 3D reality.

And then I received $50,000 which enabled me to joyously begin writing the energy alerts and have so much fun. I continue with them to this day.

Sometimes it's not easy when our parents have the old 3D work ethic standards. They may think we are lazy when we spend eight hours a month writing, and the rest of the time playing and basking...the whole while having all our needs met and infringing upon no one. This new way of being can take some time to get used to. We have been trained otherwise.

Another phenomenon that is occurring relating to letting go of our 3D jobs involves the roles of the male and female. They are reversing. As the way of the New World involves a strong emphasis on the feminine, this energy is leading the way and needs to be supported. Many men are now supporting the women so that they do not need to "work". Women need to be freed up to bring to the planet what they need to bring. This needs to be their primary focus. Until we are no longer in a monetary based society, this role of the male as the bread winner is vitally important. And it is not the old paradigm where the man works and the woman supports *him* in all other ways. Although all situations vary, many women are finding that they need this financial freedom to fulfill the roles that they came to fill for the benefit of the planet. And many men do not seem to mind a bit. At higher levels, their souls know that this will be their role for awhile.

Part of being in this space is being able to receive without any strings or complicated energy entanglements. If you can say "thank you" very simply when you are offered something, then that is all that is necessary. One time I remember being given some chocolate while in a mall. A business was giving out samples and I *love* chocolate! My first impulse was to decline because I felt an obligation to then buy something. I was stuck in the old 3D reality of energy exchange and responsibility. It does not matter where our supports come from, as energy only has the meaning that we choose to place on it. Now when I am offered a large sum of money or much of anything else, I joyously just say "thank you!" In the higher realms, you do not need to give or produce in order to get. Remember, we are simply *being*. Supports can come for any reason and from any source.

I Feel Sneaky, But...

Part of our evolutionary process involves "the New ethics", or should I say "taking things into our own hands". If you are a person who has always considered yourself to be highly ethical, this stage can seem like a conflict for you, but none-the-less, it is a part of the evolutionary process. Ethical people usually want to do the right thing. If rules exist, they are usually inclined to follow them...they like to be respectful and may also like working as a team.

With the outside world no longer a very close match to how many of us are vibrating on the inside, a conflict can arise. I rented a house recently from a property management company. To me, their ethics were atrocious. They charged several exorbitant *non-refundable* deposits and expected a lot out of me, but gave back very little. Money was their main concern and my house had not even been seen by its' owner as it was purchased entirely for investment purposes. One of the non-refundable deposits was $300 per pet and I had two cats. For most of my life, I have always been respectful, upfront and honest. I like to have good relationships with the people I do business with. For the first time ever, I went a different route. I did not mention that I had cats. I felt that the property managers were inappropriate. An excellent tenant all my life, I had always done my part, but this was just too much. Hard for me to rationalize in the beginning, I eventually felt pretty good about my actions.

When I moved into this house, it needed to have the phone line connected to the outside phone pole. This required many hoops to jump through, various approvals and signatures, and lots of waiting around. The phone company went ahead and installed the underground line for me right away. They said, "We shouldn't be doing this, but..." There were many instances that seemed to end up this way. I was told, "I shouldn't do this, but..." We cannot live within the fear and money-based structures anymore. Even the phone company decided to take matters into their own hands so they could at least provide a service.

Our outside structures and systems no longer work. It is time for them to end. They have gone as far as they can, gotten as crazy and ridiculous as possible, and now many people are not willing to operate within them. Many are simply taking matters into their own hands. Through the ascension process, a New World will be created that most of us can resonate with. Doing what we want, irregardless of what we are asked to do, may seem unusual and strange for us at first, but all in all, it is the higher road. It is time for us to set the New pace for the New reality.

Say That Again?

• The main theme or process of ascension involves letting go or *undoing* all that has been created before. The perfect ascension mantra is "give it up, give it up, give it up".

• When we undo, let go, or purge and release, we are emptying out and leaving much more room for Source to enter and fill us up. We are also returning to our original purified and pristine state....the state that we arrived in when our souls were first created.

• The ascension process is providing us with many opportunities to let go, as we cannot do it through will of the mind....we must experience it in full living color which creates a new state of *being*. The most common ways of letting go are through:

- Intolerance and apathy
- Darkness and contrast
- A dark night of the soul
- Exhaustion
- Energy shifts
- A health crisis
- Loss of employment
- Not participating in the old systems

But there is much, much more to letting go and arriving in a higher state of being. This transmutation process of vibrating higher and evolving creates some strange, intense, and at times frightening experiences for most of us. And thus come the *ascension symptoms*.

4

THE ASCENSION SYMPTOMS

HAVE YOU EVER been in the middle of a compelling conversation and suddenly you could not remember or access the simplest of words or names? Do you find yourself eating several times a day, as your blood sugar levels feel as though they are plummeting? Have you had periods where you could not sleep all night or maybe awakened regularly between 2 and 4 a.m...or also had periods where you slept like a log all night and during the day could not keep your eyelids open?

Or perhaps you intermittently experience overwhelming feelings of no sense of place. Ever looked in the mirror and not know who in the world you are looking at? Have you had periods of time where you have lost all your passion, felt deflated and lethargic, could not muster up the energy to do a thing, and simply did not care anymore?

If you have experienced any of these scenarios, you are most certainly not alone. For most of us, the ascension symptoms are perhaps the most universal, yet at the same time, the most baffling and frightening as well. With no frame of reference for what we are experiencing, we may even feel that we are developing some kind of mental disorder, or really losing it. In fact, this is basically true, as we are losing it! We are losing all the denser and lower vibrating aspects of ourselves.

Many times going to a doctor can prove futile as the mainstream medical community has not seen and has no reference for most of these symptoms. The majority of the time, the symptoms eventually go away on their own without any kind of treatment. But there are also times when seeing a doctor can be beneficial as well. And always remember, that not all our strange and uncomfortable physical, mental, and spiritual maladies can be attributed to ascension symptoms. Sometimes a cigar is simply just a cigar.

Although the ascension symptoms vary from individual to individual, many of them are fairly universal. If you are having a strange symptom or experience that is not listed here, you are not alone. Each of us is wired differently and will experience this rapid and intense process according to who we are, how we view things, what we believe, and how connected and open we are to Source and the higher dimensions.

What we believe determines how we run our energy. The filter that we run our energy through, or what we are about, will greatly affect and determine our ascension process. One of the greatest and easiest things we can do to promote a gentler ascension process is to *not take things personally*. This process cannot be avoided. We agreed to it because we knew we could handle it, and we are all in this together. Nothing is attacking you personally. You are not being abandoned, stomped on, ignored, or punished. You have not done anything wrong. You are not a bad person. On the contrary, you are having this experience because of the grand and exquisite person that you are! Your bravery, strength, and dedication are very highly revered by every living thing in the universe. This monumental experience of ascension is a unique, powerful, and amazing experience that is paving the way for all others to follow. By breaking the new ground, you are making things much easier for all who come after you. Bless you...as you are truly divine.

And know that as you progress through your ascension process, your inner child and your ego begin to diminish. In this way, the process becomes much, much easier as time goes on. You will arrive at a place, if you haven't already, where you will be able to simply observe what is going on within you from the outside. "Oh, another symptom is here," you may think or "here comes another energy surge!" As the ascension process is so on-going, you will eventually become so familiar with all its' aspects that it is really no big deal anymore. As you hobble around half dead, you get used to it (smile)! And you will come to learn that it will not kill you. You may be dying while you are alive and may feel downright strange and uncomfortable at times, but these feelings always pass. And as we are so gradually moving into all the feel good energy and feel good states of being, things get better and better. In the beginning, our density and the density of the planet is being broken up and moving out. Because it is up and around us, this is all we see and experience for awhile. But it gets better and better... and we have made so much progress already! In the end you will find that it is all worth it.

Generally speaking, our bodies, minds, and spirits are going to higher levels. They are losing their density. In order to "die" or go to a higher dimension where the frequencies are much higher, one has to "fit". You can't put a square peg into a round hole. And you can't squeeze a dense blob of energy through a delicate screen. While making this amazing transition into the higher realms while in a physical body, much is taking place as we are transmuting, so to speak. And as we raise our frequencies higher and higher (lighter matter vibrates at a higher rate), we are at times here in this old 3D reality and at times in a higher dimension.

In the higher dimensions, things are very different. We aren't used to being there while we are still inhabiting our old 3D vehicle, with an old 3D mind and way of thinking. And the physical level is always the last to be affected and to change when any kind of change occurs. And *much* change is occurring!

So then, our *bodies* are transmuting and becoming lighter and lighter and purer and purer. This can cause many various physical aches and pains as anything vibrating lower (especially old traumas and injuries or even unbalanced health situations) feel it the most. When the higher energy moves in, and we are receiving higher and higher energy every day, it affects anything that is of a lower vibration. And the lower the vibration, the more it is felt.

Our *minds* are beginning to see new realities and higher ways of being and living through this process. As the layer of density that has clouded our thinking becomes thinner and thinner, it is as if we gain great clarity and insights and can finally see what really is...and at times, we may not know where we are! Through this process, our *emotions* are also affected. When we suddenly begin to *open*, it can be quite dramatic and quite unfamiliar to us. And our *spirits* are becoming closer and closer to Source as we begin to remember what it is all about. Heightened levels of love, compassion, and gratitude are some of the aspects of the ascension process that I enjoy the most.

Because we are returning to Source and the original purified version of our souls, much is involved in the undoing process. What an exciting adventure and wild ride it is!

Symptoms, Symptoms, and More Symptoms

Although the ascension process produces many strange and uncomfortable symptoms, I have found it best not to focus on them too much, if at all possible. As most of us know, the more we focus on anything, the more it becomes a part of our reality. And in these New and higher vibrating times we find ourselves in, what we focus upon becomes more real, intense, and much more of our reality than ever before.

The symptoms are listed here so that you can validate your own personal experience and know that you are not alone, not going crazy, and not desperately ill. You are simply morphing into a human angel and higher vibrating being. Without the ascension symptoms, we may never have known for sure that we were truly ascending. Anyone who has not had these experiences themselves could most likely never understand them. But they all have a good reason and purpose along with a higher level explanation. May a giggle or laugh envelope you as you read the pages that follow...

> **1.   *Feeling as if you are in a pressure cooker or in intense energy; feeling stress.*** This is one of the first ascension symptoms that a person usually feels. In the beginning, when the energy shifts arrive, they bring with them a New and higher vibration. Old patterns, behaviors, and beliefs are being pushed to the

surface for release. Feeling all this pressure going on inside of you can feel like great stress or that you are on overload. If you are still in a conventional life with mainstream pressures, this New energy can really add to your pile. You will eventually adjust to this higher vibration and much will be activated for release within you as well. More room inside for more of the higher energy!

2. **Depression.** This symptom is most definitely in the top three and very widely experienced. The ascension process purges so much of the darker and denser energies from us, that we find ourselves *in them* for quite some time. We may feel like things are simply *never* going to get better. And to add insult to injury, the outer world is no longer in alignment with the new higher vibrating you. It doesn't feel so good out there and it may feel like there is nowhere to go that does. Therefore, everything around us feels just plain ugly and icky. And in addition, when we are vibrating higher and have to wait for the outside to manifest itself in a higher way of being, it can feel like it is taking *forever*. Feeling let down and that things will never change are so very common. This is a long process. An upside down reality, world and human are both having to turn rightside up. There is a jewel in the length of the process, though, and a necessary and perfectly intended by-product. We cannot create from the ego. We have to get to a place where we are OK no matter what is going on. Feeling disappointment for what seems like *forever* eventually makes us realize that we will never get anything that we feel we cannot live without. When we learn to detach and release all attachments, we always get precisely what we want. It is like magic and a very key part of the ascension process to let go of all attachments. When we arrive in this space, we are truly in heaven as absolutely nothing can affect us here and we also get whatever we desire, even though we desire nothing. This is a true symptom of "arriving" and one can only feel total peace from this point on.

3.   *Anxiety, panic, and feelings of hysteria.* When our egos begin to depart, they literally freak out as they do not want to cease to exist. It may feel as if everything is ending (most of everything is!). Your system is also on overload and you may feel as if you are hyperventilating. Things are happening to you that you may not understand. You are also losing behavior patterns of a lower vibration that you developed for survival in 3D. This may make you feel vulnerable and powerless. These patterns and behaviors you are losing are not needed in the higher realms.   When we experience death in a 3D world, we can panic and have anxiety as we do not know where we are going. When I went through a big leap, I knew I was "going".   My non-physical ascension guide told me to trust and relax, as it was really quite peaceful on the other side. None-the-less, with no frame of reference, it was difficult. Now, I totally trust and go with all of it and it greatly helps. When you finally "arrive" you will eventually feel much love, safety, and unity. Just wait! And also know that others are going where you are going...you are not going alone.

4.   *A need to eat often along with what feels like attacks of low blood sugar. A craving for protein.* This is another one of the first symptoms that is felt by many. Our bodies are using up an incredible amount of fuel for this process. As we are literally being turned inside out, every ounce of energy we have is being utilized. I have found it best to eat the protein along with being still during this time. These low blood sugar periods come and go for several years, but get much better as our bodies begin adjusting.

5.   *Weight gain, especially in the abdominal area.* Weight gain has been experienced and reported by *many*. It's interesting that many of the ascension symptoms greatly mock menopausal symptoms, except that many men are having them too! I have found that the abdominal area is a great protector for the solar plexus. With our internal vibrations beginning to rise, the outside world feels pretty horrendous at times. Whenever I am in the outside world, I notice that my belly seems to expand. There are some who believe that as we reach higher states of consciousness, we get a "Buddha belly". These individuals take great pride in their swollen bellies! (I prefer a flat and trim one, myself...) But all over weight gain is common as well. As we lose more and more of our density, we subconsciously fear that we will disappear and want some extra weight. In addition, this extra weight is very beneficial in keeping us grounded and supports us in processing and holding these New higher vibrations. No matter what you do, from intense and regular exercise to fasting, *this extra weight will not come off* because it is not supposed to. It is here to help us. It took me two years, but I finally got used to it.

6.   *Unusual aches and pains throughout different parts of your body.* This is another of the most common symptoms. Manifesting just about anywhere, this is a sign of purifying and releasing blocked energy that is vibrating at a 3D level while other parts of us are vibrating higher. You may feel pain in various areas of your body for several weeks and then it will simply vanish with no explanation.

7.   Continual neck and upper back stiffness and pain. We are sprouting angel wings and this is where they are emerging. Sounds a bit crazy or fairy tale-ish, but this is a reality. Our spines are vibrating differently and also connecting to a higher form of light. This area of our body is where it all happens.

8.   Headaches. It may sound strange, but our heads need to expand to embody a more evolved higher consciousness. Sinus pain is very common as well. Many times, we will experience a great amount of energy arriving through our crown chakras and this can result in lots of pressure in our heads and sinus area.

9.   Allergies. "If I am evolving so much, why are my allergies getting worse?" you may wonder. When the outside is vibrating much lower than we are, we naturally put up a resistance. Our bodies go into their usual thing that they do when they feel an invader is at large. Ugh!

10.   Skin eruptions and diarrhea. Acne, rashes and hives, etc. usually arrive when we are in the purging process and adjusting to a higher energy. Rashes are fairly common and diarrhea is an on-going purging symptom for many. At times, diarrhea can last for weeks and even months. If a doctor visit proves you are OK, fiber can really help until this phase ends. And during it all, you *still* won't lose weight!

11. **Heart pain and palpitations.** These symptoms are common for many. Our hearts are trying to accommodate a new and higher frequency. At times you can feel as though you are having a heart attack. When I experienced this phase, I had to literally lie still as any movement added too much stress to my already overstressed heart. An ER visit assured me that all was OK, but it certainly did not feel like it. In addition, whenever I had a lower vibrational thought or fear during this time, my heart would literally grip and stop beating. It was wild, but not a medical condition, and it eventually passed. Our hearts are where we will be coming from and connecting from in the New World and they must be in alignment as well.

12. **Gritty eyes and blurred vision.** Very simply, our eyes are adjusting to see in a new way, in a higher dimension and new reality.

13. **Waking up at night between 2 and 4 am. As you progress, waking every morning at 5 am.** So much is going on at higher levels that we cannot be "out there" for very long. We need to be back in our bodies. My personal theory has to do with dimensional access and I really believe this to be true. In the beginning, we wake up regularly between 2 and 4 am. And we are very wide awake for several hours. We are accessing dimensions and arriving through these dimensional portals when we awake. As we are releasing much in the beginning and need to go "back" to everywhere we have ever been, we begin at the lower dimensions. Eventually we wake up or enter at 5 am or in the 5th dimension. After our critical mass evolutionary leap in January, 2006, I never woke up in the morning until 12:00 noon! I must sound like a very lazy person, but ascension has a lot to do with the number "3" and this number began to get *very* prevalent for me. If I forced myself to wake up earlier, I felt very out of alignment and completely off. Before that it was 10:30 every morning. I just hope I get to start waking up earlier at some point in the future!

14.   *Periods of very deep sleeping.* When the energy is not moving and we are done for awhile, we get to rest. While we are integrating and preparing for the next phase of intense moving energy, we become very lethargic. It can become near impossible to keep your eyelids open in the daylight hours and daytime napping can become a regular and necessary habit. Even if you think you can exercise your way back to some energy, you will usually find yourself dropping dead on the sofa at every effort.

15.   *Experiencing emotional ups and downs; weeping.* Our emotions are what carries the energy. When we are falling apart (and we are doing just that), we can get pretty emotional. When we are releasing, we can cry at the drop of a hat. A sad movie can make us cry, or even a sad commercial. We can cry when we experience kindness. We can cry when we feel relief. We can cry when we see any kind of suffering. The tears are a great cleanser and releaser. I always know when some New energy has arrived because I can simply cry while I am driving along in the car. This seems to be an on-going symptom that is here to stay for awhile. But at least it is fairly painless!

16.   *Night sweats and hot flashes.* During certain phases of ascension our bodies suddenly decide that they are going to burn off the lower and denser aspects of ourselves. You may wake up in the night soaking wet or become very hot during the day. It may be 35 degrees outside, but you are just fine and dandy in your short sleeves.

17.   *Feeling cold with an inability to get warm.* When we are moving into a much higher dimension after much integrating, detoxing, and other ascension processes, we get very cold. We are in between and preparing to move up. At these times, it can be very difficult to warm up no matter what you do. I usually submerge myself in a tub of hot water and then get under a heavy comforter.

18.   *Vivid, wild and sometimes violent dreams.* We are releasing many lifetimes of lower vibrational energy through our dreams. If you are one who usually receives their higher information through dreams, you will most likely do a lot of releasing at night. I consider you to be lucky, as some are doing much of their releasing while they are wide awake. These dreams usually do not make sense, but if you are good at dream analysis you can usually figure them out. These acid-trip like dreams are up and visible because they contain energy that is on its' way out, never to return. Through this process, we are releasing all of our past lives.

19.   *Dizziness, loss of balance, vertigo, and spinning.* The definition of Merkabah is: Counter rotating fields of light surrounding the spirit/body which serve to transport the spirit/body from one dimension to another. And this is precisely what is occurring. As we connect to our light bodies and begin moving into a higher dimension, we begin spinning and can experience vertigo and dizziness. If you know that this symptom indicates that something wonderful is occurring, it can feel great and actually be quite fun...like a roller coaster ride.

20.   *Overall body pain and days of extreme fatigue.* Our bodies are morphing into a crystalline form in order to enable us to reside in the higher realms and to continually be able to receive the higher light. This process is on-going as it cannot happen overnight. If you feel as though you are 100 years old and barely able to walk across a room, this is why. Continual fatigue is also an on-going symptom for the same reasons. We are losing our density and going through extreme restructuring.

21.   *Severe bloating and indigestion.* When the energy surges occur, many experience severe bloating as they are greatly expanding. This can be on-going but is intermittent.

22.   *Memory loss and difficulty accessing words.* So many are having this symptom that we can only laugh as we try to converse with each other. "I was having a glass of...you know what I mean...that white stuff...uh...what's it called?" "Did you watch the...er...that event where everyone competes from around the world?" At times we cannot even talk at all because we are simply unable to access much of anything. When this occurs, you are going back and forth between dimensions and experiencing a disconnect. Another somewhat related occurrence is trying to type words and having the letters become jumbled in the wrong order. In this case, we are not in alignment with time and our flow is disconnected as part of our energy is here and another part is further ahead.

23.   *Difficulty remembering what you did or who you talked to a day or sometimes just an hour before.* In the higher realms, reality is very much in the moment. If we do not hold something in our consciousness, it simply ceases to exist. We have no attachments. We are creating our own world around us through our beliefs and thoughts and what we do not hold onto does not exist. Everything is brand new as we are starting completely over, moment to moment. We can tap into whatever we choose to at any moment and create and experience just that. This state comes and goes, but is practice for living in the higher realms. It can feel a bit creepy when it occurs. In addition, at times we are neither here nor there, as we are in between dimensions. This phenomenon can occur at this time as well.

24.   *Not remembering the meaning of anything.* When I was in an intense period of the transitional process and we were in the throws of a substantial energy thrust into the higher realms, I remember looking at a trashcan and not knowing what it was for. I had to access my memory of the "old" and reach far. What was happening was that I was vibrating at a point where everything possesses only the meaning and identity that we give it. In the higher realms, energy is just energy with no label or meaning. All is fresh and new. Sort of a *Course In Miracles* undoing process, without the trying.

25.   A feeling of disorientation; not knowing where you are; a loss of a sense of place. "Where in the world am I? I do not fit anywhere and nothing seems to fit or feel remotely right! And I do not know where I belong or where I am going or what I am supposed to be doing either!"   Ever had this conversation with the universe?   You have been knocked out of your old grooves by an energy shift and are in between realities.   You have successfully left much behind and are in a very new space but have not integrated yet. You won't have much time to integrate, though, because as soon as you get comfortable you will be moving on into the next higher vibrating space. And in addition, the outside world does not remotely match the way you are now highly vibrating.

26.   A loss of identity. You look in the mirror and have a strange feeling of disconnect as you no longer recognize that once familiar image. You almost feel out of body. Once this phenomenon occurs it never ends. You have released so much of your ego self, that you are no longer the same person, and do not have that attachment or connection to your physical vessel. As you begin to access much more of your soul or higher self, you are not in your body much. You may still use your voice to communicate and other bodily aspects, but   you   are   slowly   beginning   the   process   of disappearing and releasing the human form. In addition, you have cleared much of your old patterns and are now embodying much more light and a simpler, more purified divine you. All is in order...you are OK.

27.   *Feeling "out of body".* The same explanation as above. The physical body is the last to catch up. Much of us is now in a higher dimension and residing outside of our bodies, as our bodies are not there yet. They are much denser.

28.   *"Seeing" and "hearing" things.* As we can now access different dimensions fairly easily, it is common for many to see things moving out of the corner of their eyes or hear things when nothing is there. Many also experience a ringing in the ears, which is common when we are going through "the tunnel" and accessing a higher dimension. Depending upon how sensitive you are and how you are wired, this can become a common experience. Many are seeing orbs and vibrating blobs of color as well.

29.   *Heightened sensitivities to your surroundings. Crowds, noise, foods, TV, other human voices, and various other stimulations are barely tolerable. You also overwhelm very easily and become easily overstimulated*. You are tuning up! Know that this will eventually pass. During the ascension process we become highly sensitive. At one point, I could literally feel the vibration of the chicken when I tried to eat an egg. In addition, you may find that you are unable to eat in restaurants or be in a store and feel like running out of them as fast as you can.

30. ***Feeling you are going insane, or must be developing a mental illness of some sort.*** We are rapidly experiencing several dimensions and greatly opening. Much is available to us now. You are just not used to it. Your awareness has been heightened and your barriers are gone. This will pass and you will eventually feel very at Home like you have never felt before, as Home is now here.

31. ***Feeling as though you are looking down a long tunnel in order to connect to lower vibrations; feeling as though you are acting or pretending.*** When we are residing in the higher realms, anything not there with us may feel far away. If you are still in a lifestyle where you are regularly interacting with the outside or old world, you may feel like an actor in a play or that you are pretending your way through the day. Basically, you are no longer residing in that world, even though you are still involved in it.

32. ***An intolerance for lower vibrational things (of the 3D) reflected in conversations, attitudes, societal structures, healing modalities, etc. They literally make you feel "sick" inside.*** When we begin arriving in the higher realms and in a higher vibration, our energies are no longer in alignment with the old outside 3D world. Through a severe intolerance to the old, we are being "pushed" to move forward...to *be* and create the New. In addition, you may feel like staying home or just being alone as much of everything "out there" no longer matches the higher vibration of YOU. This is simply a very common experience of evolution. We are moving forward before the outside manifestations are. Being in the old can feel downright awful. It is similar to having to "go back" after you have had a near death experience. As the ascension process continues, going back to the lower dimensions will not feel good nor will it be possible for long, as it is difficult to drop our vibrations down in order to reside there. This is a simple experience of navigating the dimensional hierarchies. We will eventually become experts with our dimensional navigational skills.

33.   *You don't feel like doing anything.* When we feel like this, we are in a rest period, rebooting. Your body knows what it needs. During this time you may feel as though you have lost your passion and joy and don't know what in the world you want to do with your life and don't really care! This phase occurs when we are realigning. At higher levels, much is realigning as well. Things are being put into position so that all will be ready when you move forward again. In addition, when we begin reaching the higher realms, *doing* and *making things happen* becomes obsolete as the New energies support the feminine of basking, receiving, creating, self-care, and nurturing. Ask the Universe to *bring* you what you want while you cannot do it for yourself. And know that you are always being taken care of during the ascension process, even if it does not feel like it at times. Those in the physical going through this process are very highly revered by all of the cosmos. We are most certainly being watched over.

34.   *A wanting to go "home" as if everything is OVER and you don't belong here anymore.* As we are returning to Source, everything *is* over. (But many of us are staying to experience and create the New World.) Also, our old plans for coming have been completed. We are basically done with our prior incarnation that involved raising the frequency of the planet with a goal of reaching critical mass. We achieved a lot of this through transmuting the darker and denser energies through *ourselves*. Now we don't have to do that anymore and may feel like we simply want out of here and away from that experience. What is coming next is simply divine and does not remotely resemble the first phase.

35. A sudden disappearance of friends, activities, habits, jobs and residences. One of the most basic and prevalent experiences in the higher realms involves the Law of Attraction. Like energies always attract like and similar energies. This relates to the dimensional hierarchies as well. We will always be matched with what and how we are vibrating. As we go higher and higher, this phenomenon becomes much more magnified and also becomes one of the basic cores of our reality and existence. Through the ascension process, we are evolving beyond what we used to be, and therefore the people and surroundings that no longer match our vibration simply leave our space. This can sometimes occur rather dramatically or at times through a simple desire resulting from an inability to relate to them like we used to. When an energy shift occurs, it can feel as though a bomb has been dropped and everything in our world has been scattered from here to there. Eventually we realign with the New. When the New arrives, you will feel so-o-o-o much better!

36. *You absolutely cannot do certain things anymore. When you try to do your usual routine and activities, it feels downright awful.* Same as above. You are no longer a fit and it's time to move on to a much higher vibrating way of living, being, and creating.

37. *Your plans suddenly change in mid-stream and go in a completely different direction.* When this occurs, your soul is balancing out your energy. It usually feels *great* in this new direction, as your soul knows more than you do! Your soul is breaking your rut choices and vibration. Our souls always know more than we do. During January of 2006, we experienced what I dubbed "ascension shock". At higher soul levels we had a specific plan and timeline. If we were a bit behind, we ended up experiencing our pre-plan whether we were ready or not. This placed us in sudden and immediate new circumstances so that we would be poised for what we needed to do next. I remember suddenly relocating from Flagstaff, Arizona to a remote small town in Northeastern Arizona. I new I would be residing there one day, but not yet! As time passed, I could eventually see how perfect it was, but following my soul and not my ego was a bit of a challenge. Now I am eternally grateful and in total bliss.

38. *You have created a situation that seems like your worst nightmare, with many "worst nightmare" aspects to it.* This experience is similar to above but not quite the same. Your soul is guiding you to stretch aspects of yourself where you were lacking, or tone down aspects where you had an overabundance. Your energy is just balancing itself. Finding your way to peace through this situation is the test you have set up for yourself. This is *your* journey, and your soul would not have set it up if you weren't ready. You are the one who finds your way out and you will. Looking back, you will have gratitude for the experience and be a different person.

39.   *You are alone and don't want to be.* Part of ascension involves losing the fear of being alone. We all have it...a fear of being alone. But before we release all attachments and enter the higher realms, we have to come to terms and create peace with being alone. Therefore, we have to experience being alone in order to create a stronger connection to Source and especially to ourselves. During this time, we really have an opportunity to find out who we are.   After we complete this process and are no longer afraid of being alone, we get to be with everyone!

40.   *Feeling as if you are sinking into a deep hole and you will never be able to get up and out.* There are many ways to experience this phenomenon. Some feel it physically as if they are losing themselves and falling into a great abyss. When they lie down, they feel as though they are literally falling. Some experience it during dreamtime. For the most part, it manifests as a very *sinking* feeling and it can sometimes feel terrifying. This experience relates to the dimensional shifting going on. When we are "in between", as we are so much in the beginning stages of ascension, many strange and unsettling things can occur. During this time, we are in no man's land, but it passes. This was a big one for me and freaked me out when it occurred. But as we progress, this particular symptom no longer occurs.

So Many Symptoms and Then None

The majority of the ascension symptoms occur when we are going through "the tunnel", or rather the transitional phase from one dimension to another. After we have finally made it through, most of these symptoms completely disappear, and then you find yourself wondering what everything was about in the first place!

As the ascension process continues on, you may feel periodic symptoms when pivotal points arrive in the form of energy shifts or planetary alignments. The further you have gone in your process, the easier the process becomes. Those that are coming along behind you may feel intense symptoms during these pivotal shifts, while you may simply only be mildly aware of them, as they are supporting you while you are still moving ahead. You have integrated much and are now much more aligned. After many have caught up to you, you will then move into much higher levels of "morphing". Basically, you have been restored and now can move into the higher states of being. This is where it can really get fun as you begin to actually become a higher level being with unusual abilities.

At times in the beginning, you may feel as though you will never survive this process, but know that there is an end to the first phase. And after you have completed much of it, you will feel stronger and more connected than ever before. Your inner child will not be running the show, you will feel grounded and connected to Earth and sky while embodying much of your higher self or soul. Also know that the ascension process will continue on for a very long time. Stretching and losing the denser aspects of yourself will become a way of being...especially during the bigger shifts.

But there are some things that can ease the process a bit. And trying them can at the very least distract you from your woes and convince you that things can indeed get better.

5

———

TOOLS FOR COMFORT

"SOMETHING TERRIBLE must be wrong with me." "I think I am dying." "This is the strangest thing I have ever experienced." "I think I am losing my mind." "Any doctor would think I am crazy and never understand." "I am losing my foothold and can't seem to get it together." "I *really* don't fit in now. Why is everyone else going along fine in their lives, and I am having these weird and unsettling feelings and emotions?" "I don't belong here anymore." "What *else* could possibly happen?" "I can't take anymore." "I'm all alone." "No one else understands." "Everyone else is in some other place having another experience and I am…I know not where, but it is neither here nor there." "I feel just plain strange." "Things in the world are seemingly getting worse and worse and nothing seems to *ever* change or get better." "I am so confused. Nothing makes any sense anymore and I don't know what is going on with anything."

Hmmmmmm...how about some more thoughts: "Wow. Everyone I know is experiencing hell. I'm sure glad I'm done with that." "I've never felt so much peace and freedom in my life. I feel as though I am away from all the yucky stuff." "It's sure calm here. I feel at one with nature and the cosmos, and so very connected and powerful." "Every night I sleep like a baby." "I never want for anything. All my needs are always met. I feel so protected, safe, and taken care of." "I get to be in my passion 24/7. Every element of my life involves being in my creativity and just *being*." "I have such a simple life. I am not attached or connected to anything." "I love having no agenda and I don't have to be in an appointment based reality anymore. I love being able to do whatever I want to whenever I want to. I can't imagine living a box-like structured lifestyle!" "I'm sure glad I got out of *that* relationship." "When I look back, I can hardly remember the person I was or the life I was in."

If you haven't already, you will go from paragraph one to paragraph two. It can be hard to imagine the reality of paragraph two when you are in paragraph one. When we are really *in* a space, it can feel as though that is all there is. But things *always* pass. Some tools for comfort are listed below in order to lessen the experiences of paragraph one, but even if they weren't, there are two basic facts that may help the most during the ascension process:

Each And Every One Of Us Is Being Monitored And Watched Over

We are absolutely not alone with this. The non-physical being that I speak to the most and who is with me daily now, first arrived shortly before I broke my leg. He was so *huge* and solid and ancient and quiet that I did not speak to him often. I was not yet resonating and vibrating where he was, but he arrived for a good reason. He (actually there is no gender, but I will just say "he" for simplicity) knew what was about to occur and he knew about the ascension process long before I did. Even though many times I was not aware of it, he was with me every step of the way. He would show up when I was at my wits end and say the very thing I needed to hear. Eventually I began to see him and hear him more often, and now that we are at much more of the same level, he is my constant companion. He says that we are in this together as we are helping each other. He is so advanced and from such a far away place, that my friend who is a gifted psychic medium can barely hear him and he will rarely reveal himself to her or allow her to connect with him. He has assisted in setting up and choreographing many things when I was barely functioning. And in dangerous situations, he never leaves my side as he provides a barrier of protection.

I tell you this because each and every one of us has an "ascension guide" who is with them always. This also includes our animal friends. These guides dutifully make sure that our process is going smoothly and that nothing goes awry. Even though we may feel that things have gone out of control and that we are so very helpless, know that this is not the case. Our "guides" will be with us for awhile. They are vibrating very high and they are very "advanced." Eventually we will be perfectly matched and then we will surpass them and be guiding them. For in actuality, we are only interacting with higher aspects of ourselves. It's just more fun to put them in a form and have a story and drama to be a part of! And it doesn't make us feel so alone, either. We just don't yet realize how grand we actually are, so we place our grandness outside of ourselves.

During my last big ascension leap, I was feeling very "not right" and decided to drive myself to the hospital. I wanted to know for sure if there was some sort of physical problem going on that was very real. I was there for four days. During that time I had a thorough examination and discovered that I had a very real chemical imbalance due to some remedies that I had gone on and off of too quickly and too radically, along with some big ascension shifting. My ascension guide had told me this, so I believed it. I had consulted several healers and alternative doctors, tried various holistic remedies, and just plain needed some allopathic medication. Muscle testing had proven to be inaccurate (as it indicates what the person being tested believes), as was much of anything else. I tell you this because help can come in any form. Resisting medication was something that hurt me in the long-run. Taking a relatively unheard of low dose of a medication is what saved me and got me back on track.

While in the hospital, several nurses came to my room individually. One told me that I was releasing many past lives. She said that she had recently gone through something similar and found it best to allow the waves of energy to flow through you instead of resisting them. This was a very mainstream large hospital (St. Joseph's) in Asheville, North Carolina. Another said that I was taking on the energy of the other patients and I needed to be careful. She also told me to place white light around myself. A late night nurse said that she had been experiencing insomnia also, and had tried every herb out there and was now taking a tranquilizer, much to her chagrin, but she desperately needed relief. She also gave me some herbal recommendations, but requested that I tell no one about it.

After I was released, I received a phone call from the hospital regarding my bill. Not having been in the system for so long and rarely experiencing poor health, I had no insurance. I called the hospital back, ready to set up some kind of solution. They replied that they were only calling to tell me that I need not pay my bill. It would be taken care of and I also did not need to fill out any forms. My new doctor that I needed to see outside of the hospital, decided to treat me for free...just because. And the nurse at this new doctor's office said that she had been experiencing many ascension symptoms herself and had gotten by through being in the moment and placing white light around herself.

Know that we are always being provided for, even if it feels otherwise. We are being lovingly watched over from above (actually, it's not really above, but *through*) and are deeply cared about. We are greatly assisting everything in the cosmos by being the ones who are experiencing ascension in the physical...we are all in this together. The other thing to know that can greatly help is:

Placing Yourself In Higher Realms Energy As Much As Possible Greatly Supports The Process

The majority of the time that we are feeling out of whack and miserable is because we are misaligned and in the process of re-aligning. One of the easiest and sure-fire ways to experience some sort of relief is to connect to a higher pocket of energy. This places us in the higher realms and greatly assists to lessening the feelings of the lower and denser energies that are leaving us.

During the ascension process you may not be able to meditate. Or you may have never meditated. I am personally not a meditator and feel great. Meditating doesn't open up any new doors for me. But there are other ways to be in higher level spaces while being involved in the world. The easiest is through your creativity. If you can, begin to investigate different kinds of creative outlets that seem like something you might enjoy...or simply spend more time in your already existing creative outlet. These activities serve to get us out of the way and to allow that uninterrupted stream of Source energy to flow through us. We are also contributing through our creations, as well as greatly aligning with the New World and connecting more deeply to the part of us that will remain after much of the releasing and cleansing is completed. Being in our creativity also distracts us from any unpleasantness we may be going through. Whatever we are focusing on then becomes much more of our reality.

If you are too uncomfortable to do anything creative, another way to connect is through the earth. The earth and nature have the ability to balance us and bring us back to it all. Be out in nature as much as you possibly can. Soak up the sun, walk on the beach, or in the forest, or simply sit out on your deck and commune with the birds if that is all you are able to do. Another incredible remedy is to lie on the earth. If we never did anything else in regard to our personal wellness, this might indeed be enough. Lying on the earth daily calms us down, balances us out, and reconnects us in a special way. The energy she possesses is truly amazing and absolutely free. And in the winter months you can use a tarp and bundle yourself up.

Spending time in nature at elevations above 7,000 feet can accentuate your nature and Earth experience. Or simply spending time above 7,000 feet alone can make a difference. At the higher elevations we are above the consciousness and it is therefore, much clearer there. I have lived a fair amount of my adult life above 7,000 feet and it really helps as I do not pick up much energy from the outside world.

Being with the animals and the little ones in human form (our beautiful children) are also wonderful ways to get out of yourself and connect higher. When I didn't know who I was for awhile and could no longer do much of anything, I would go to my granddaughter Amayah's preschool and play with all the three year-olds. We had so much fun sliding, playing in the sand and running. I don't know who had more fun, them or me! And when we weren't doing that, we were going on walks with all the kids in the family, jumping in mud puddles, and ooing and aahing at just about everything. The ascension process brings us back to our original innocence and this is where it is at. My daughter used to (and still does!) get so exasperated with me as my granddaughter and I would have so many adventures and get into so much trouble, but deep down she was happy to see all the joy and fun we were having.

Animals can be great too as they simply think we are crazy and don't know why in the world we do what we do. I spent a lot of time lying on the ground with my cat, being in the moment, and experiencing her world. And now I feel part feline as I love to lie down in the sun in the afternoons and simply *be*.

All of the remedies above are still a great part of my everyday living experience. Now they are not remedies, but simply a way of being. Below are some other supports that can truly help during this time. And you may have found many more on your own not listed here that really work for you as well.

1. ***Rest. Rest. Rest.*** Your body is going through an incredible transformation and is on over-load. For those highly sensitive with fragile nervous systems, rest can make all the difference. I have found that severely limiting my activities and attending to extreme self-care has made a considerable difference. It also has a natural by-product of putting you in the higher realms of simply *being*.

2. ***Water is key.*** Perhaps the most helpful support for the body is water. It cleanses us, neutralizes us, and has many other attributes yet to be discovered. Drink lots and lots of it, submerge yourself in it and move through it (preferably a pool)...and program it through your intention to do what you desire. My ascension guide told me at one point to submerge myself in a pool on a regular basis and move through the water; not just sit in it. For some reason the water acts as a buffer and neutralizes our ascension discomfort. Right about this time, a friend of mine called from another state and told me that she had been reading a very popular ascension book. The chanelled being in the book had suggested swimming in a pool to alleviate ascension symptoms!

3. ***Soak up magnesium or salt water.*** I still do this on a regular basis. Magnesium or salt can greatly help nearly anything that ails us. Several times a week I take a bath in magnesium oil. I use MSM lotion and soap as it absorbs through the skin as well. And I put MSM in my drinking water. Many have reported the benefits of swimming regularly in salt water...especially the ocean. A natural part of our bodies and the earth, the ocean is great for supporting and restoring ourselves.

4.   *Let your soul guide you and let go.* We tend to want to be in control of what is going on and may over do grasping for some kind of relief. If you let go and ask, your soul will bring to you the messages you need (whether through another person, a book, an e-mail, etc.), and is a great navigator for a smoother and more pleasant transition. I have found that less is more. The process itself has its own way of getting you where you need to go, and you can easily over-stimulate yourself by trying to take charge or through over remedy-ing yourself. Letting go in all forms is one of the key supports for ascension. Holding on to the familiar only serves to cause much more discomfort. You will have to let go eventually, so why not do it earlier than later and have more ease. If I had not totally given up during my hospital experience, I may not have received all the help that I did. Others certainly knew more than I did. Your information and help will come to you much more readily if you get out of the way. And you will have much more room in your being for the light, if you agree to let go of much of yourself and your old life. ***Trust, trust and trust some more.***

5.   *Exercise.* It greatly helps to keep the energy moving. At times it can be difficult to exercise when we are so completely exhausted and feel as though we are 100 years old, but even a daily walk can make a difference.

6.   *Try not to resist the process.* The first five supports are really the forerunners here, but there are still some other tools that can help as well. Resistance blocks any flow of Source energy. Being in the flow can really help and resistance can be a detriment to our well being in any situation. If you can allow the ascension process to do what it needs to do and trust that all is well, it can greatly ease the process. When we accept and understand this process, and know we are being greatly helped, even though it may not feel like it, we then harmonize with the process and it becomes much less severe.

7.   *Monitor your thoughts.* Higher and positive thoughts will immediately place you in the higher realms, as well as assist greatly in what you are creating. Find a *feel good* vision for yourself and use it often. I frequently envision my perfect life in all ways. Know it will arrive. You have the vision because you are supposed to be living it! And as we now find ourselves in these New and higher vibrations, what we think about becomes very real for us indeed.

8.   *If you are guided to supplemental support, take it.* When we are on overload, adrenal support can greatly help. Herbs for relaxing are good as well. And as I personally found out, if you feel that medication is needed, don't be afraid to go that route. As our bodies are continually being thrown out of balance, you may have a hormonal imbalance, a thyroid imbalance, or the possibility of many other health situations that can benefit from a doctor's diagnosis. When I broke my leg, my orthopedic surgeon actually wrote me a prescription for Reiki, even though I had to explain to him what it was! Many allopathic doctors are really coming around.

9.   *In the beginning, find a support system and use it regularly.* When we are falling apart through the ascension process, we really need supports.   Mainstream therapy or counseling can greatly help with the inner child aspects that come up for release. Acupuncture can help to keep the energy flowing and in balance and it tells your body that all is well. And gentle yoga stretching or kundalini yoga really connects one to the higher realms. It has a way of going through several layers and also keeps one grounded. Whatever form of support that resonates with you is a great help in the beginning stages. Even EFT assists with releasing.   But after you reach a certain point, any kind of healing will greatly short circuit things for you. Healing will no longer fit you in any way as you are now vibrating beyond it. You will know when this occurs as you can really feel this great change within you.

10.   *If you are experiencing hypersensitivity, alter your lifestyle in regard to crowds, excitement, and stress.* As you evolve, this will eventually become a permanent lifestyle for you. Your life will become *simple* and you will no longer crave input from the outside as you are now very connected through your inner and higher self.

11.   *Visit or connect with friends and simply listen to their day.* Remember, you are "emptying out" much of your identity, and you may be able to contribute very little at times. It greatly helps to stay connected to others, even if you think you don't want to be around people. It wlll also get your mind off your own process. I would frequently call my mother and just listen to her talk about her day. It was comforting to know that someone out there was having a normal and stable life.

12. Stay as grounded as possible and maintain healthy boundaries. When we are opening to a higher dimension, it can throw off our normal sense of navigation and reality. Staying grounded can really help. The earth herself is ascending, so if you anchor into her you won't be left behind. In addition, it is quite possible to go into an even higher realm than we may want to. Stay anchored to the earth. There is a lot of energy flying around out there that is being released which is not you. Maintaining healthy boundaries is very important during times of ascension. As the old, dense energetic walls are coming down, our old boundary structures are leaving as well. In the higher realms, the boundaries are very thin and are basically composed of thought and intent. Until we are very familiar with this new structure, maintaining healthy boundaries is a must.

13. Find endless ways to make yourself feel good. Read a good book (something fun, not heavy or "spiritual"!), walk in nature, take a bath, get a feel good massage, buy a new car, get a new wardrobe, take an art class you've always wanted to take, get your hair done, go to a spa, redecorate! Feeling good is vital, and the universe will in turn support you, as you support yourself. If the universe knows you are all about feeling good, it will follow along. This is our natural state of being and also places us in the higher realms! When you let the universe know that you come first, it will bring you what you need.

14.   Make a personal declaration about how you would like your own ascension process to unfold. You are the master here, and we need not feel like victims. As you evolve, you will eventually remember the tools to control your own process and experiences.

15.   Be in the moment. If all else fails, simply be in the moment. Let everything go and simply love yourself and all others. You will eventually end up here anyway, so why not practice now?

As we are leaving so much behind, we may not feel that we are good for much anymore. We may feel that we have nothing left to contribute and our self-worth can become affected. What we are really leaving behind is our ego, or who we thought we were and how we thought we needed to be. When much has left us, what remains is the pure gold nugget of our true selves, shining ever so brightly. What we thought was our power, very simply was not. Our connection to Source and our true selves is our real power. As we begin moving ever so swiftly into the higher realms and higher ways of being, things can be very different indeed. And the higher realms may not be entirely what we had expected.

6

BEGINNING EXPERIENCES
IN THE HIGHER REALMS

IMAGINE WAKING UP each morning to bands of angels hovering all around you and brilliant music filling your ears. As you rest on beautiful puffy, floating clouds, you don't have a care in the world. Popping one bon bon into your mouth at a time, you ponder about what you would like to experience next. You have finished all your "life lessons", completed all your "karma", finished your "contracts", and suffered your way to heaven because you finally "earned" it.

If you are here in this scenario, you are most likely not in the higher realms.

Everything that I have shared with you throughout this book comes from my own personal experiences in the higher realms and the process of getting there, as well as any multidimensional traveling I have done. Nothing here comes from books, channelings, or conversations with higher level beings. As I came to know over time, things were simply not what we had been told because...they were much, much better.

And why, then, should you believe me? You shouldn't. Everyone's experiences are different because we each create surroundings and realities that come from within us. And this alone pretty much sums up the higher realms; the higher realms come from *within*.

As the ascension process serves to release and purge much inside of us that is not of the light, we then begin to experience much more of a higher way. It is a very natural process and a beautiful one at that. As much of the density begins to be cleared away, a great and shiny clarity is revealed that, if you let it, can serve as a perfect roadmap for being in the higher realms.

This chapter lists some interesting experiences you may be having upon reaching a higher vibrating reality. But generally speaking, reaching a higher vibrating reality involves finally seeing clearly what really is. It is not interacting with other energy forms and experiences through your ego or inner child. It is not being attached to anything but Source. It is simply *being* and experiencing energy.

Below is a list of new ways of being that usually arrive when we begin to reside in a new and higher vibrating reality. Many of these greatly surprised me as they were so much simpler and *better* than I could have ever imagined. The old rules and ways we were told of the higher realms were derived from an ego-based consciousness that existed behind the veil, and were some of them ever wrong! And the majority, but not all, of any channelings only derive from the individual who is channeling the information. Anyone can tap into any energy pocket they choose that is vibrating as they are and get about any kind of information that matches their belief system. Who knows about the accuracy. Through the ascension process, we *go there*. In this way, it is quite different indeed.

1. ***You reach a certain level through your ascension process where you no longer desire or resonate with any kind of healing.*** And like a reformed smoker, you can get frustrated when the New Age arena continues to focus much of their energy on healing. As we begin to vibrate higher, we no longer need healing. Healing serves to basically introduce us to a lower vibrating energy that is no longer any kind of a match to us. It can take us "back" where we no longer are. And it can *really* bring in a lower vibrating energy that we need not ever focus on again. Where we place our energy and focus greatly becomes our surrounding reality more than ever in the higher realms. Why would one want to continually focus on lower vibrating energy? This energy can feel like something from another world where you are no longer residing. And receiving a healing after you have "gotten here" can also short circuit your system.

2. ***You no longer have the same connection with your physical family.*** We chose to be born into a physical environment in order to support the development of necessary traits that we chose to embody in order to support our soul purpose. In addition, most of us agreed to uplift the planetary vibration through transmuting the darker and denser energies. After our prior incarnation is complete and we are done and have arrived in a higher realm, our purposes with our families are now obsolete. The cords are basically severed. We are no longer connected through issues. We are done with this experience. Therefore, our family members can suddenly disappear from our lives for no apparent reason as there is no longer a connection to them. But if we continue to simply love them and have that as our connection, we can continue to maintain a relationship based on joy and choice. And after we arrive in a higher state of clarity, we are also able to clearly see who they really are and how they operate, which has absolutely nothing to do with us.

3.   *Your lifetime friends suddenly leave your life.* Same as above. And sometimes we re-unite with friends we haven't seen for eons. And this energetic pattern is also true for geographical areas on the planet as well. When we are done with a particular purpose, we are done. In the higher realms it is all about joy, fun, experiencing, and creating with no attachments. This is why we may also get to go back to old friends and geographical homes as we are now uniting for a different purpose.

4.   *You suddenly see what it is all about and always has been and it has nothing to do with "karma", "contracts", "life lessons", or "Earth as a school".* These are things that someone made up and many of us bought into. We needed a story to explain why we were so uncomfortable and we needed it to be spiritual and purposeful so that our suffering would not be in vain. When the fog finally lifts and we rise above it, we are no longer seeing through limited thinking of a lower vibrating consciousness. It is all about energy and using it to have an experience. We wanted to play games. We made up stories. At times we came to the planet to try and alter it through our higher consciousness that we placed in form (our bodies). We were bored at times. The purpose of Earth and of existence is to create through form. We were never trying to get anywhere, continually trying to go back home. We wanted to play, have fun and experience. And we weren't serious all the time! Spirituality is about joy, fun, creating, and playing. It is absolutely not rigid, full of rules, or judgmental. It is about freedom, love, and laughter.

5.   *You are no longer interested in spiritual gatherings, group meditations, or the New Age arena in general.* You have come to realize that intentional spirituality is not really real and does not stick. The truth of the matter is, we are spiritual 24/7 no matter what we are doing. Forced spirituality removes us from the world and places us in artificial situations where we are not really *being*, but "trying" to *be*. In the higher realms, we are simply living our lives and experiencing. We are not continually wanting something else and trying to place ourselves in situations that we think may bring us closer to Source because they seem to be more spiritual. It is far better to have the presence of your being here in the world rather than in a pocket of distanced and artificial "trying".

6.   *You get rid of all your spiritual and self-help books and no longer desire to learn anything new.* Congratulations! You have arrived in the state of *being*. You are also done learning as you are readying to provide your energy through your special gifts and talents by simply being in a space where you greatly enjoying being. Being in the moment relates to this as well. And expanding and growing always comes from experience, not from book learning or mental awareness. We can now get any additional information we need through connecting directly to Source. In addition, if you are no longer craving any new information, you are most likely done in this universe and preparing to go to the next level.

7.   *You crave simplicity and can barely tolerate anything complicated.* We have released so much that we are much more in a state of simplicity. In the higher realms, one does not need to make anything happen or to do one thing in order to have an outcome. There are no hoops to jump through or complicated processes. When we are *being* a vibration, we simply and naturally draw it to us. And remember, in the higher realms we are simply being, creating, and experiencing. No planning, agendas, opinions, or having to prove something or do something in order to receive something.

8.   *Negativity feels downright awful.* In the higher realms, there is no contrast or negativity. When we reach a higher state, we know intuitively that life is about joy, passion, and creativity and we never have a thing to complain about. Negativity comes from powerlessness and this state does not exist in the higher realms. And continually talking about anything in a negative way brings it to life and makes negativity a real experience and reality. It gives it fuel and allows it to exist.

9.   *Drama is a thing of the past.* When we reach the higher states, we can clearly see that we had been most certainly existing in a "play". As we are now living and viewing things from a higher level, we no longer need dramas and stories to unfold around us due to unintentional and unconscious creating. We no longer desire this emotional state of powerlessness as it no longer fits where we are. And we are much too tired and apathetic, as a perfect by-product of the ascension process, to have the energy for this kind of thing!

10.   *What you think about seems to arrive in record time.* This effect really becomes evident during energy surges.   It is perfect training for practicing positive thinking.   We are so used to receiving realities as if from no part of our own.   We are coming to know that we can really consciously create now with purposeful intent for our best outcomes.   And having things arrive for us in record time can be a great opportunity to become very clear in all aspects regarding what we are trying to create. It can be fun to continually tweak our creations until they are perfect.

11.   *You now wonder why you used to think you had to surround yourself in white light or clear any energies.* In the higher realms this is a waste of our time. Again, it only serves to focus energy on what we do not want, thus giving it energy and making it real.   When we are vibrating high, lower energies cannot possible affect us or gain access to our space as they are not even a close match.   With like energies attracting like energies, we are now free and clear to create, enjoy, and experience. This ties in with the dimensional hierarchies as well.

12. "Saving" has no place in the higher realms. Saving anything only serves to deny it of its' rightful experience of growing and expanding and trying something new through the contrast that is spurring it on. Saving is interfering and comes from ego. If one were to check in at a higher level with the mountain, the person, or the animal that is being saved, one would surely see that all is in divine right order and these things do not need saving. I have done this many times and always with the same outcome.

13. Putting yourself first is mandatory. Plain and simple. We cannot pour from an empty pitcher. Giving yourself away is disrespectful to yourself. The best way to uplift the planet and really serve is by sharing who you are through your special passions, gifts, and talents and continually doing what you love to do. After you have mastered putting yourself first, you will naturally move on to service.

14. You no longer have the desire or need to make things happen, to "try" or to "fix" anything. At higher levels, we always know that everything is always in divine right order so nothing needs to be fixed. We also need not intentionally make things happen as simply *being* them will draw them to us along with intent. The old masculine involved doing and extending ourselves. Through the ascension process we become so weary that we cannot extend even if our ego got in the way and encouraged us to! We also know that we have to accept things and be OK where we are before we can create anything new. In the higher realms, we clearly get that we need to accept where we are and *be* there, before we can move ahead. Resistance only blocks the flow of Source energy and short circuits us.

15.   *All your needs seem to be continually and miraculously met.* At first, this space may seem strange and new, but after you get used to it, you don't expect anything else. It becomes a way of being and lasts. This occurrence is especially prevalent in regard to money. If you have reached a higher level and are really on track with your soul purpose, you will absolutely and totally be supported. I know because this has been my own personal reality for several years and I used to really struggle financially before I "arrived". This support never goes away.

16.   *You have no issues with the current people in your life.* This is similar to #2, but in the opposing direction. Your relationships will now revolve around companionship and projects with no "issue" related hooks. You love, admire, and adore each other for who you are, with no dependencies. When we get to the space of no attachments, we are then free and clear in all ways. This is where the fun, joy, and love really come in.

17.   *You no longer relate to mental and analytical processes.* In the higher realms, we interact and exist in relation to *feeling*. We come to know that we only need to feel our way to anywhere. And besides, our brains and thought processes are barely working anyway. This is the beginning of really using our intuition or rather connecting more highly with our souls or higher selves...another step in getting our ego out of the way. And in the higher realms, there is no right or wrong, good or bad, or black or white. Things either feel good (vibrating high) or they feel bad (vibrating low). Everything simply *is*.

18.   *You no longer care what anyone thinks about you.* You also may not care about what anyone thinks about *anything*! You do not care what anyone thinks about you because a lot of your ego is gone. In addition, in order to fulfill our soul purpose (which is also our passion and joy), we can't be feeling insecure or powerless with the possibility of being knocked out of our grooves from an ego posture. Becoming worn down and tired, again, gets us out of the way and we begin to say, "I simply do not care anymore!" Perfect.

19.   *You finally realize that there is no dark or light.* There is only light. All energy is always going in the same direction with a higher level purpose of supporting the light. The appearance of lack of light only exists to ignite the light or provide the contrast needed to spur us on to create and bring in more light. In the higher realms, polarity is no longer needed once we realize this and have integrated it.

20.   *Your health improves.* And this involves your physical, emotional, and mental health. With all the purging and releasing, we have literally been put back together so to speak, in a more solid way. And then, just like the earth herself, we will move forward once we have been restored. We will then begin a real "morphing" into a higher level form of human and beyond.

21. ***You get to retire.*** You begin to experience a flow to life at a slow, leisurely pace where you need not do anything you do not really wish to. Everything falls into your lap. You life consists of much basking, savoring, creativity, a strong connection to Source and gratitude for the simple things in life.

22. ***You have no agendas.*** I have not used a day planner for years. The rare times I need to make an appointment (usually for my hair!) or be somewhere at a certain time, feel extremely off and confining. One of the reasons I discontinued giving personal soul readings was because they were scheduled. In the higher realms, we naturally meet up with who and what we need to connect with through synchronicity and the Law of Attraction. Occasionally, I will find myself conversing with a stranger and end up giving them a reading...all very naturally. It's all about being in the moment and trusting.

23. ***You have no responsibilities.*** And when you do, it feels so downright awful, wrong, and confining that you can barely tolerate it. This is why the first wavers are going first as they are primarily in their 50's and their children are grown. It was all perfectly planned. To ascend, we must be totally free and clear with no attachments. After much of the purging and purifying is done (for awhile, at least), what is then left is the purer gold nugget of the real you. In the higher realms we need only wear one hat. We do not need to scatter our energies in places that are not a pure and clear reflection of who we are at the highest levels...or our soul purpose.

24. **You have no more fear.** In the higher realms we have mastered trust. Having already been through so much and come out alive, it must mean that there is a higher plan going on. Besides, we're much too tired and weary to do it all on our own anymore. At some point, we have learned to let Source in and help us out.

25. **When something unpleasant occurs, any corresponding emotions come and go in record time.** A dramatic event happens in our life and we're over it almost immediately. No holding on. Being in the higher realms is being in the moment with no attachments. We know we can start fresh and new in any given moment and create a whole new life, scenario or space to occupy. We have become masters at releasing.

26. **You are rarely connected to your surrounding environment.** Or the environment that was created from the old consciousness. You find that you spend much of your time in your own personal sanctuary at home and that you spend much more time than you ever did alone or with a very small circle of close friends. The outside world and many of its' inhabitants are not yet vibrating where you are. You just can't do it anymore and are much more comfortable out in nature or spending time with animals.

27. **You have an unquenchable thirst for creativity.** After so much has been swept away within ourselves and in our lives, we may find ourselves in a space of boredom. What do you do now that most of your needs are met and you are so very free and clear? This is when the creativity comes barreling in. In the higher vibrations, it is all about creativity. We have come into form to experience and create. When you arrive in this space, you will feel like you are almost manic with your creativity. The enormous amount of energy that is now running through you demands an outlet. And now that you are no longer in a space of healing, fixing, trying to make change, or shift the energies, it's time to have fun and create, create, and create!

28.   *You laugh a lot and find many things amusing and funny.* Lightheartedness is a natural state of being in the higher realms. Enough said.

29.   *You have a heightened love and compassion for all living things.* The higher states can at times overwhelm you, but they feel *so good*.

30.   *Incredible peace is a mainstay.* Great peace seems to be about all there is for you at times...and these times are frequent. Being still in the simplicity...watching a spider crawl down it's web in the sunshine...basking with your cats...being one with a sunset or even with a bug on the earth. All regular and frequent occurrences.

31.   *Your inner child seems to have disappeared.* Although you still love to play and frolic. In regard to childhood wounds and issues, you no longer see things from this point of view. What is now left is simply the healthy aspects of your inner child...seeing things with awe and wonderment and the original innocence. And oh, is it wonderful! This is why it can be so much more comfortable to hang out with our little ones...they get it.

32. You begin to have an understanding about how all is connected. You understand that there are no mistakes, all is in divine right order, and there is never and was never anything "wrong".

33. You are much more connected to your soul. You and your soul or higher self are now much more one. Your human personality that operated from a disconnect and from beneath the veil is seemingly no longer running the show.

Am I In Heaven?

My mother and I frequently have conversations about anything and everything. One day I was telling her that I had just discovered that absolutely *everything* comes from within, including the angels and our loving spiritual guides. They are simply aspects of ourselves that we believe in and therefore they exist. As mentioned earlier, we create them so we won't be alone. We want to feel better knowing that somewhere out there, there exists something that knows more than we do and knows that all is well, even if we don't know ourselves. We place them outside of us because we cannot imagine that we are, in fact, this wonderful and wise ourselves. She agreed that everything comes from within, but was not too happy thinking that perhaps nothing exists except what we believe and that we are making everything up. She said she felt much better believing in a reality that consisted of loving and comforting angel companions and perhaps sitting on billowing white clouds in heaven.

And this is the truth about the higher realms. Although we may be surprised about what a higher being looks and feels like as we begin morphing into one, we can always create our own heaven. If all is really an illusion and we can make it up, why not make up the perfect heaven of your dreams?

I have a close friend who is a rancher and ranching real estate broker. He is also a very ancient being and lightworker, although he isn't consciously aware of it. Several years ago we went to see the movie *What Dreams May Come* with Robin Williams. In the movie his character dies and goes to a heaven with colors everywhere and magical occurrences. Years later, my friend confided in me that he was concerned as he would not be comfortable transitioning over into this kind of world. He had been keeping this fear inside for years. "Oh my gosh!" I said to him. "Your heaven would be a beautiful ranch where you could mend fence and irrigate all day out in nature where you love to be!" And this is how it is.

If we are making everything up, we can most likely create whatever we choose when we reach the higher dimensions. A perfect manifestation of who we are. But the higher we go, the less ego we have, and our heaven involves many different things that we may not have imagined from our old ego selves. "Morphing" while in human form gives us the added beauty of creating a heaven that matches where we are at each stage of our evolutionary process. And this is reflected in the process we are going through now.

On more highly evolved planets, there exists a very conscious pattern or blueprint for energy to manifest and exist that supports a perfect harmonious interaction. There is a basic flow or order that perfectly "houses" energy to best support creation and expression. This is in relation to the energy or intentional formation of a planet. As we can now create much more easily what we are vibrating or what we want, what will the energy or blueprint for our New or restored planet Earth look like? At higher soul levels, what have the lightworkers all agreed upon as the model for the New World? What is the vision that so many of them share?

7

THE NEW WORLD

IN AUGUST OF 2005 we reached critical mass on planet Earth. So many had raised their vibrations enough through the ascension process that the earth and her inhabitants were now ready for a New reality. With the advent of this phenomenal energetic event, many felt a sudden disconnect. At some deep level within these individuals, there was a strong sense of "being done". At soul levels, a deep knowing occurred...a knowing that one very important mission had been accomplished. This event also resulted in a letting go. The vibration of the planet had finally reached a pivotal point and lightworkers (those who were here to create and greatly assist with The Shift of The Ages through their physical human form) were no longer required to hold the space of light. Lightworkers were done with their work and many felt lost. But what a success it was! Being released from one assignment then freed up many to make their next choices.

Would lightworkers stay and create the New World? Would some of them now leave through the 3D death process? Or would some even choose to stay and simply observe and experience what would happen next?

Many have chosen to stay and create the New World. Before these lightworkers can leave the current universe for other destinations, they have chosen to leave behind a very New palette for creation called the New Planet Earth. This process involves restoring the Earth to its' original blueprint; a blueprint for creating and experiencing from a higher consciousness with no interference from darker or lower vibrating energies. Once it is restored, it can then be taken to higher levels and formed according to however the inhabitants of the Earth choose it to be. What will it look like? What will the lightworkers create? What will they leave behind for all others to utilize as a playground for creating and experiencing?

When this very new phase began in 2006, it was a new beginning for many. The first half of the year involved integrating, detoxing, aligning, and setting up. The second half will involve the manifestation of the New. A rebirth was occurring for many, as those who had arrived in the higher vibrating reality of this very New World had basically been reincarnated again. They were no longer the individuals they had been in the old world and now had very new roles and purposes. And this affected friendships and relationships as well. Lightworkers were now lined up and interacting with those who would be sharing their new roles, new assignments and purposes. Many prior soul mates would be parting, but many new soul partnerships would be forming as well.

The old world roles for lightworkers involved all forms of raising the consciousness and vibration of the planet, from healing to environmental education, to challenging governmental structures. And in addition, another purpose existed for lightworkers in the old world. As mentioned before, the lightworkers had volunteered to transmute the darker and denser energies through their own physical bodies and experiences. After critical mass was reached, they would be done with this specific purpose. The ascension process had also assisting in restoring these human beings to their original and purer form. All the purging, releasing, and purifying that were experienced in earnest during the prior five years had assisted the lightworkers, as well as the planet, in reaching a point of restoration in order to begin again.

For some, their roles would remain the same but be taken to higher levels (i.e. teaching higher ways of living and being). For others, they would have entirely new roles, but be the same individual with the same unique energetic blueprint that they possessed in the old world. Many lightworkers would discontinue any kind of healing work as they were now vibrating higher than healing. Healing does not exist in the New World.

All in all, the new roles all involve the creation of the New. No trying to save old structures, trying to save people, or trying to change and fix things. With the advent of 2006, it was now time to create the very New palette and the New Planet Earth.

So what does this very new palette look like?

The New World Model

There is a central theme that all energy revolves around. If we were to go back to the very beginning of creation, this theme would be present there as well. Imagine a central hub of energy called creation. From out of this creation hub come various off-shoots or legs of energy. These legs are all still connected to the hub as they share, and will always share, the vibration of the central hub. But each leg also has its' own unique energy as well, as it has left the hub and is now vibrating a bit differently.

The original blueprint for Earth shares this energetic theme, as do all other forms of creation. The earth is also a leg as well as a central hub. In regard to the earth as a hub, there will exist cities (or legs) of light, all sharing the same vibration of the hub (the earth), as well as having their own unique vibrations. Each city has its' own special, unique, and significant vibration or purpose. Each of these cities contributes its' own unique vibration to make up the whole of the planet, as well as containing the energy of the planet itself. The cities are also all connected to each other in order to support the planet. *Briefly:* The Earth is a central hub with its' own purpose and theme. It has extending legs that are cities of light. Each city shares the purpose and theme of the earth. Each city is connected to all other cities of light.

The energetic theme or blueprint for *each city* is again, the same as for all creation. Each city will be a central hub itself with its' own individual theme that contributes to the main theme of planet Earth. The center of each city will also contain the higher vibrating frequency of Source and the earth herself. Each city will also have legs that vibrate uniquely, but also share the main energetic theme of the city. The legs of each city are the individuals who reside there. They all share the same theme or purpose of the city. This manifests within each individual as sharing the same purpose and passion. In addition, each resident will have their own very unique purpose and passion, that when combined with other residents, make up and contribute to the theme of the city, which in turn contributes to the theme or vibration of the earth, which in turn contributes to the theme or vibration of the solar system, and so on. In other words, a microcosm. Whew! *Briefly:* Each city has at its' core (or center) a connection to Source. Each city also has its' own unique purpose and theme. Each resident shares the same purpose and theme as the city. Each resident also possesses a unique theme or passion that contributes to and supports the theme of the city.

Your Very Real Experience

Imagine being very aware of who you are. You ARE your special gifts and talents. You naturally vibrate them. They are effortless for you. You love who you are and are simply *being*. You don't vibrate exactly like anyone else. Your particular energy is unique to you...a perfect compilation of your incredible gifts and talents which result in a *beingness* that only you possess. No one expresses their particular gift in exactly the same way that you do. You wake up each morning joyful to be alive. You cannot wait to be and do what you came to be and do. You have a passion and joy for where you choose to direct your vibration...for what, how, and where you choose to create. The opportunities for expansion and creation are never ending.

You live in a community where all is in harmony and balance. Your particular community has, at its hub, a particular vibration that you resonate with. There are other communities on your beautiful planet and each have their own particular vibration, or theme. Each community is in vibratory resonance with that same unique vibrational identity of the geographical spot on Earth it is located upon. You are very connected with those in your community, as they belong to your soul family. You remember and know each other well. You have a great love, caring, and appreciation for your family as you have been together since time began. You are joyful to be in each other's presence. You are known for who you are and how you vibrate, so when your community needs that niche filled, you are naturally the one to fill it. It is expected that you will, as you are highly revered for who you are, and your vibration naturally completes the perfect harmony and balance of your community. You don't need to be "off" and "on", as you are continually *being* and doing your gifts, talents, joy, and passion, all effortlessly. You are in perfect alignment with Source energy.

Your community interacts in perfect harmony with nature, the nature spirits, with the planets, and with all of life. All is represented, needed, appreciated, and accepted. What is not needed does not exist, as there would be no need to create it and it could therefore, not be sustained through thought and experience. Your community utilizes and flows with the energy of the planetary alignments, as they are part of the whole as well. You each have a specific and individual vibration along with the identical vibration of the whole. Everyone and everything has a perfect niche and all is effortless. Your needs are continually met at all times, therefore there is never an experience of using up your energy in a direction that does not support the expression of YOU. Source energy flows with no resistance, as you realize that you are yourself, an extension of Source. There is regular communication and visitation with light beings and beings from other dimensions. Higher knowledge is easily accessible and experiencing other worlds is a common occurrence. You are all united in the same goal and moving in the same direction, with no need for resistance of any kind, creating a continual channel for Source energy. You are all one.

Art and creation abound. Quality hand made works of art fill your home and enhance your environment. You feel good just having them around you. They raise you up. These creations are a contribution of each individual's sharing and expression of who they are, as are yours. Architecture is magnificent. There are water wheels, windmills, and unusual ways to harness the ever abundant energy that surrounds you. All structural creations are in perfect harmony and alignment with nature. There is no monetary system, as everything needed is fulfilled by someone expressing and being their gifts and talents, their passion and joy. All is freely given. To live in your community, you need only to be, to express, and to allow. *Being* who you are at the deepest level (from your soul), *expressing* through your creations, and *allowing* source energy to pour through you.

I'm A Salmon?

When each and every one of us has come to a certain point in our ascension process, and when we are activated according to the current frequency of the planet, we will then migrate to our geographical home on Earth. Like a salmon swimming upstream, your soul will simply know when it is time to go. Some will be very conscious of this event, while others will arrive at their geographical home for another reason seemingly not related to this divinely guided purpose. But you will be there, and that is all that matters. And when you arrive, it feels absolutely divine. You will be a total match to the energy of this location on Earth and you will *finally* feel as though you are home. You will be here, not because you are needed to balance the energies within or without, but because you are ready to create something that is a total manifestation of what you are all about and totally aligned with. And your geographical home on Earth will be in total alignment with you as well. All in perfection, bliss and divine right order.

Before these cities of light can be created, each individual and each area must be restored to its' original pristine condition. Just as we are going through the ascension process of purging, releasing, and cleansing, so is the earth and your specific geographical place on her. The timing is always perfection. Some will arrive early and others will arrive later, all according to each individual's purpose in relation to his/her city. If you are a set up person who is continually ahead of the game and who continually finds yourself paving the way for others, you will be the first to arrive. If your continued role in your community involves connecting energies far and wide, you will arrive first. If your role has always been in creating foundations in harmony and balance, you will arrive first. If your passion and gifts involve creating beautiful art, you will arrive as things progress and your gift and contribution is needed, and so forth.

No More "Working"?

In the higher realms we always have everything we need. In the New World all our needs will be met in two ways:

> 1. Each resident of each community will be contributing to the perfect and harmonious functioning of the community through their unique and special passion and gift. This is the gift of who they are after they have completed much of their cleansing and purging through the ascension process. What we do not contribute ourselves will be contributed through another. And each of us will simply be *being*, *being* who we are with no effort required. Anything not being contributed through the existence of another's passion and creations will not be needed, as there cannot exist a need without a person to fulfill it. Passions for

passions, joys for joys, and all in total bliss and connection to Source.

2.   Our needs will also be met through our total connection and alignment with the earth and the cosmos. Every existing thing in the universe has a unique vibration and affects and contributes to the whole. As we learn to live in these communities in total alignment with the planets and celestial bodies (the sun and the moon), they will support creation in another way. The earth contains all we need to survive upon her. We have forgotten how to utilize her gifts. We have become disconnected. We will be learning many new ways to harvest our needs through her resources as we will be part of her. Other ways of creating will be utilized as well and they all have to do with *alignment*. Becoming one with the earth will be vital and necessary component. Much more will be said about this in future *Life In The Higher Realms* books, as this is a whole new story on its' own!

As the New World begins to form, many will be having experiences that will serve to encourage them in "arriving". The old structures will really begin to fall and malfunction at the precise time that many will be feeling a strong desire to do something different. This is how evolution and creation occurs. All at the same time. Old jobs and careers will begin to falter, as there will suddenly occur a time of getting no business or receiving no money. This is an indication that you are no longer residing in that reality. You are not being supported because you have moved up a notch and are now vibrating somewhere else. You have a different and higher role. For healers, your business may suddenly dry up as you are now vibrating beyond the need to give or receive healings. Healing does not exist in the higher realms...remember?

And when structures and business that were created in the old world reality can no longer serve us (as there are too many hoops to jump through and they all revolve around money and the way of giving in order to get, etc.), many will literally have to create another way of surviving. The New World depicted in the paragraphs above is certainly the highest way, but as the process begins unfolding, many steps will arrive first. Most inhabitants of the earth are not lightworkers, therefore, they will progress much slower and at a rate and reality that better suits what they believe can happen. No judgment here as lightworkers have always been a breed of their own, but virtually everyone will eventually no longer be interested in "the old". It will simply no longer feel right or good and this will create a yearning or wandering into something else. This is a part of the letting go.

Can I Come In *Yet*?

Because the lightworkers have come to lead the way and assist others in "arriving" in a new and higher vibrating reality, they will be the first to begin creating this New World with these new communities of light. These communities will then be firmly established and ready for anyone else to arrive. When we *believe* in something, it then becomes real for us. As many more begin to become willing to let go of the old, as it has gotten unbearable and unmanageable, they will then begin to be ready to *believe* in and let in something new. And as all creation exists within dimensional hierarchies, individuals will begin to arrive in these communities when they are matching the vibrations of these higher realities. Remember, no access granted anywhere until we are *being* where or what we want!

Although many have held the vision of a higher vibrating planet for some time now, it is quite different when it finally begins to arrive. You see, we had to *be* it before we could create it. And as we are being supported and watched over by all of the cosmos, this is a very exciting time indeed.

Arriving in this space of the New World can leave some debris in our paths as well as a sense of great loss, even though we may finally feel that we are somewhere New. How do we know that we are on track and that we are indeed connected?

8

OUR ETERNAL CONNECTION

BECAUSE THE ASCENSION process creates so much loss, we can at times feel very disconnected. Our sense of security can really go through the ringer. Through this process we lose friends, family members, jobs, our old (ego) identity, our old source of financial support, our old homes, and on and on. The list can seem endless at times. And even those whom we considered our closest soul mates can end up with "another assignment" or perhaps no longer match our new vibration anymore and leave our space as well.

We can easily become confused, lost, fearful, disoriented, and feel as though our barometer has gone awry. But there is one way to really stay on track when all else fails. When it is time to make a change, (and in these times we are making changes every five minutes as we are "morphing" so fast!) we become discontented with where we are. Our work, our living situations or even perhaps our entire lives no longer feel good. This is the nudge that is guiding us to make a change. And the way to guide yourself through this change is to do what makes *you feel good*. It's that simple.

If something no longer feels good to you and is not working for you anymore, discontinue it as soon as you are comfortable doing so. It is no longer working because you are no longer in that space. Something new is waiting for you. If we were to stay in the old space out of mental rationalization, the new opportunities and manifestations could not find us. If there is something you always wanted to do but didn't think it made sense to do, do it anyway. If you do not know what to do, then fill as much of your day with things that make you feel great and the new will arrive on its' own. Always, always put yourself first. Follow your heart. Make time for you and the universe will get the picture.

In this way we are always connected. When the denser and darker energies are leaving it can feel uncomfortable at times. But if you can find ways to stay in the higher vibrations and higher realms through what makes you feel good, you will greatly assist yourself in staying in alignment. Certain things feel good to us because we are *supposed* to be involved with them. And even when you find the good feeling things, you will always need to "tweak" them on a regular basis until they are in their purest form (i.e. new publishers or ways to get out your writing, higher ways to present your music and art, etc.). We will need to tweak things until we are at the point where we are only wearing our one hat...not spending any of our time consumed with other responsibilities.

This is one of the reasons why the ascension process places us in a space where we can become disenchanted with life. We are only supposed to be in our passion and in the energies that light us up. Stay in these as much as possible. We are becoming the pure gold nugget of our true selves and this does not include being the accountant, sales rep, e-mail sorter, or planner (unless that is your passion, of course). It was intended for us to be our purest vibration of our contribution and our creativity. And this is where we are headed.

I have days where I do not feel like writing, even though I absolutely love it. On these days I paint furniture, sew, or simply spend the day in nature. These are my other passions. And I can and need to do this, even if I *should* be writing. I have had to learn that nothing will go awry or fall apart if I take a time out for me. Actually, it is just the reverse. If we are doing what we love because we think we have to in order to make money, it will not work. We have to know that we will be provided for. Our mindset is very important here. Financial support does not need to come from any kind of supply and receive situation. When our usual passion ceases to be fun and bring us joy, it is either time to tweak it or to shift gears and do things only for the fun of them while we allow everything else to fall into place. I am frequently asked to do radio interviews, but unless I feel like they will just be fun with no agenda (like book selling), I will not do them. (I rarely do them...I would rather be out in nature!) And this applies to promoting as well. If you stay in your creativity and bliss, everything will *come to you* on its' own.

Am I suggesting that you go sit on a rock and wait for everything to fall into your lap? Of course not. This is a process and it involves trial and error while we are learning these very New ways.

Our eternal connection also relates to individuals in our lives. For many of us, there are certain people who simply feel like home. When we are feeling discombobulated, lost and fearful, the simple sound of their voice can bring us back home and center us in record time. With so many instances of being knocked out of our old grooves and now vibrating higher than everything around us, we can so very easily feel like we do not fit or belong anywhere. Nothing feels remotely good or right. These individuals can bring us back home and connect us once again. In this way, we never lose our connection. And many times we are unable to be a regular part of these people's lives in a physical "being together" sense.

At higher levels, we were "created" at the same time that these individuals were. This is why we feel this strong connection that seems unbreakable. And it *is* absolutely unbreakable. Although we may be vibrating at different levels in the human sense or have consequently taken on different assignments according to what we agreed to do, know that we will most certainly be re-united in the end. Our connection is eternal and we will absolutely be together again.

We have soul connections that relate to projects, as well as soul connections that come from our hearts. These very deep connections from the heart are what I would consider twin flame connections and they come with a devotion to one another that is never ending. By having these people in our lives in some capacity, we can feel eternally connected even when we are feeling just the opposite.

Another way that I regularly feel connected is through the non-physical beings that I spend so much time with. I have to say, I am very selective and feel the best when I am with the highest vibrating of them all. And these are the only ones that I allow in my space! These beings are incredibly loving, have incredible knowledge and wisdom, cherish the ground I walk on, and just plain feel good when they are around. So we are back to the basics again...realizing that feeling good is being connected.

Although the ascension process can make us wonder if it is all worth it or question if we even want to remain on this earth, the rewards are truly worth it in the end. If we hang in there and are willing to let go and explore new territory while getting out of our own way, we may just find ourselves in a place of near bliss and deep connection to Spirit, while we are truly living in the Promised Land.

As this unusual process continues on, we still have a very long way to go. But the more we progress and the higher we vibrate, the easier it gets. If you were to look back to who you were only a few years or even month ago, you would most likely be amazed at who you have become.

While the process continues on step by step, we are all in this together. We are having such similar experiences because we are all one and connected through the very same energy. As brothers and sisters we are creating a brand New universe for all others to utilize and enjoy. And we are creating it through ourselves.

Are you ready to live in harmony and alignment with your passion and joy and who you *really* are? Are you ready to be much more connected to Source? Are you ready to have a life of expansion into new and higher vibrating realities?

May this book have served as a guide to ignite within you what you already knew and to inspire you to know that you are always right where you need to be. Until next time,

Karen

About The Author

Karen Bishop is the creator of *What's Up On Planet Earth?*, a website devoted to the ascension process and life in the higher realms. Recognized as an authority on ascension, Karen has reached thousands of readers worldwide through her weekly energy alerts about human and planetary evolution, along with the latest information about ascension symptoms and our current planetary status, since 2002.

A life-long clairvoyant, multidimensional traveler and communicator, she has also undergone the challenges of the ascension process . Inspired to use her gifts and talents to reach others going through this amazing on-going evolutionary experience, she continues to give the latest information of our ascension process and life in the higher realms through her mini book series and website.

With an educational background in psychology, counseling and law, Karen has served as a facilitator, counselor and teacher, working with county agencies, non-profit agencies, Native American tribes, public school systems and various individuals.

Currently residing in Springerville, Arizona, she follows her joy and passion through writing, sewing fabric art for home interiors (now as a hobby), enjoying her animals and time in nature, and communicating and experiencing the higher realms. She is currently working on her mini book series *Life In The Higher Realms*.

For more information about Karen and her latest messages and writings about the ascension process and life in the higher realms, please visit her website at:

www.whatsuponplanetearth.com. You may contact Karen through her website.